Other Critical Essays

William Faulkner: An Estimate of His Contribu-
tion to the Modern American Novel
by Mary Cooper Robb $1.80

The Fiction of J. D. Salinger
by Frederick L. Gwynn and Joseph L. Blotner . $1.50

Henry Miller: Expatriate
by Annette Kar Baxter $2.50

The Fiction of John O'Hara
by E. Russell Carson $1.25

James Gould Cozzens: Novelist of Intellect
by Harry John Mooney, Jr. $2.00

The Hero in Hemingway's Short Stories
by Joseph DeFalco $2.00

Entrances to Dylan Thomas' Poetry
by Ralph Maud $2.00

The Short Stories of Ambrose Bierce: A Study in
Polarity
by Stuart C. Woodruff $2.25

Joyce Cary

Joyce Cary

The Comedy of Freedom

by

CHARLES G. HOFFMANN

The University of Pittsburgh Press

For Tess

PREFACE

*W*hile in England during 1960–61, I examined the entire James M. Osborn Collection of Joyce Cary manuscripts in the Bodleian Library with the kind permission of Mrs. Winifred Davin, literary advisor to the estate of Joyce Cary. The Osborn Collection, consisting of nearly 300 boxes of manuscripts and some 250 notebooks, contains all of the extant manuscript versions, working notes, and notebooks of Cary's works, fiction and nonfiction, poetry and plays, both published and unpublished, completed and incomplete.

The Osborn Collection is a detailed record of the genesis and development of Cary as a novelist. It is a fascinating writer's workshop, a kind of practical journal of his methods of writing, ideas for characters, plots, themes, and scenes. The various versions of the published novels reveal the genesis of each novel, and the unpublished and usually incomplete manuscripts of novels contained in the collection reveal important steps in Cary's development as a novelist. Cary experimented with ideas and scenes for novels, and it is this unpublished material which provides the sense of continuity in his career as a writer rather than his short stories which, except for some very early stories written for popular magazines under a pseudonym, were mostly published in the 1950's. Though some parallelism of theme and character, particularly in the African material, is to be found in the short stories, Cary never sufficiently developed his talents in the short story form. His genius needed the scope of the novel to develop.

Until recently Cary, though a major novelist, has been

largely neglected by the critics. There have been some excellent short studies of Cary's novels. One of the best of these is Walter Allen's short monograph, *Joyce Cary*. It is especially perceptive on the first trilogy, particularly in its discussion of *To Be a Pilgrim*. Barbara Hardy's excellent essay, "Form in Joyce Cary's Novels," illuminates Cary's method of counterpointing the past and the present in *To Be a Pilgrim* and *The Moonlight*. Hazard Adams' essays on the two trilogies show the specific interrelationship of the three "voices" in each of the novels of the trilogies. However, until Andrew Wright's book, *Joyce Cary: A Preface to His Novels*, appeared in 1958, no major study of Cary had been made. Although Professor Wright examined some of the manuscripts while Cary was alive and subsequently catalogued all of them for the Bodleian Library, his study is limited in its discussion of the significance of the manuscript material and its relationship to the published novels. Robert Bloom's book on Cary's novels, *The Indeterminate World* (1962), came to my attention after I had completed writing this manuscript. Though a full-length study, Professor Bloom's book is limited by its thesis approach to the novels, that all of Cary's fiction, and particularly the trilogies, suffer from his indeterminate view of reality which deprives the novels of a moral center but which at the same time provides them with their source of strength, multiplicity.

I wish to acknowledge the kind and courteous help the librarians of the Bodleian Library gave me while I worked on the Cary manuscripts. I take this opportunity also to express my gratitude to Mrs. Winifred Davin for the generous and gracious offer of her time and help in answering my questions about Joyce Cary and about the manuscript collection. Her suggestions and criticism were very helpful in the writing of this study. I wish also to thank Mr. Roland Gant, then an editor for Michael Joseph, Ltd., for allowing me to examine Joyce Cary's correspondence concerning the second trilogy. It is with his permission and that of Michael Joseph, Ltd., that I quote Cary's letter on *Except the Lord.* I acknowledge with appreciation the research grant-in-aid from the University of Rhode Island for work on this manuscript. I wish to acknowledge Curtis Brown, Ltd., and the estate of Joyce Cary for their kind permission to quote from the James M. Osborn Collection of Joyce Cary manuscripts.

For their permission to use revised versions of my articles, I wish to acknowledge the following journals: *Modern Fiction Studies, PMLA* (by permission of the Modern Language Association), *South Atlantic Quarterly* (from material copyrighted 1963, Duke University Press), *Texas Studies in Literature and Language, University of Kansas City Review,* and *Western Humanities Review.*

CONTENTS

I "Change Itself Is My Country" 1

II "There's a War On": The African Novels . 8
Aissa Saved
An American Visitor
The African Witch
Mister Johnson

III "They Want to Be Happy" 44
Castle Corner

IV "The Child Is a Born Creator" 54
Charley Is My Darling
A House of Children

V "Freedom as Creation": The First Trilogy . 67
Herself Surprised
To Be a Pilgrim
The Horse's Mouth

VI "The Fearful Joy Is Love" 99
The Moonlight
A Fearful Joy

VII "Politics Is the Art of Human Relations":
The Second Trilogy 127
Prisoner of Grace
Except the Lord
Not Honour More

VIII "The Free *Perceive* Their Captivity" . . . 157
The Captive and the Free

Notes 171

Bibliography 199

Index 203

CHAPTER I

"CHANGE ITSELF IS MY COUNTRY"

*W*hen Joyce Cary began to write the prefaces for the Carfax edition (1951–52) of his novels, he considered writing a general preface to the whole series under the title, "Comedy of Freedom." In looking back on his novels, he saw a thematic pattern: "My novels," he wrote in a letter, "are all about one world—as much so as Blake's poetry is about his world and I want, like him, to make people feel that world which might be described as that of freedom." He sought to create "a homogeneous picture of the world as it is, as [the]perpetual creation of the free soul with all its complex results in art and religion and its politics, its special tragedy and special morality." [1] Cary eventually abandoned the idea of a general preface, but certainly all of his novels are about the world of freedom, a world of perpetual change. "Change itself is my country," Cary wrote in another letter, and it is the idea of change as freedom that is the underlying theme of his novels. Thus the free soul stands before all possibilities, creating his own special world in art, religion, and politics. The comedy of freedom is the joy of creation itself, but the very act of freedom brings with it responsibility for its consequences whether for good or evil. Paradoxically, the tragedy of freedom—injustice in the world—is an inevitable corollary of the comedy of freedom, for the free act may create evil as well as good.

In a more special sense the theme of freedom is the unifying concept of Cary's early approach to the multiple novel form in the African novels and in the projected *Castle Corner* series. The multiple novel as a literary form

1

is a series of interrelated novels having a unifying theme and a structural unity. It may use a single narrator throughout the series to give it unity (C. P. Snow's *Strangers and Brothers* and Anthony Powell's *The Music of Time*), or it may use more than one point of view to give a multiple view of reality (Cary's two trilogies and Lawrence Durrell's *Alexandria Quartet*). It may use the history of a family to give an interlocking unity (Zola's *Rougon-Macquart*, Galsworthy's *Forsyte Saga*, and Cary's *Castle Corner* series). It may have a unifying concept to give structural unity: Balzac's *La Comèdie Humaine* is a comprehensive commentary on all aspects of French society and life, and Cary's African novels are a complex exploration of different aspects of the war between religions and cultures in Africa.

Joyce Cary wrote in the multiple novel form throughout his literary career and contributed significantly to its development as a literary genre and to its theory as a literary form. The James Osborn Collection of Joyce Cary manuscripts in the Bodleian Library reveals Cary's intention of developing the African novels as a series. In a draft of a letter to the publisher of his first novel, *Aissa Saved*, Cary wrote:

> I have written several books with this theme [the "war of cultures or religions"] or parts of it, for a general background or atmosphere. . . . All these plots are what might be called old fashioned or dramatic, and they are worked out in action, not only because such plots suit my purpose by shewing nature in contrast but because what I want to portray and convey is not to be grasped, any more than any other kind of reality, by the brain alone, in contemplation, but only by a combination [of] thought and feeling. I meant at one time to call this series of books of which several are in construction "There's a war on," as a general title; or something of that kind, since they all deal with this theme of war between incompatible ideals.[2]

The African novels form a series in which the underlying theme of a "war between incompatible ideals" in

relation to the setting remains constant. Each novel contributes its exploration of an aspect of this war so that
the whole series is a complex, interrelated examination of
the revolution that took place in the early part of the
twentieth century (and is taking place today) in Africa.
Though the main characters change from novel to novel
—Bradgate (*Aissa Saved*) and Bewsher (*An American
Visitor*) are mentioned in *The African Witch*, but they
do not appear as characters—the colonial officials can be
viewed as representing the various attitudes of the colonial mind related to the exploration of the several aspects
of the general theme. Similarly, the main African characters can be viewed as representing different facets of
the African mind. Thus, these novels are interrelated by
the part each character contributes to the over-all theme
of the series, the war of ideas.

The Osborn Collection also contains Cary's notes and
trial scenes for the incompleted and unfinished volumes
of the *Castle Corner* series: *Over the Top* and *Green
Jerusalem. Castle Corner*, as originally planned, was to
be the first novel in a three- or four-novel series, but after
the unfavorable critical reception of this first novel, Cary
abandoned the project. It is evident that Cary intended
this series to be a family chronicle tracing the history of
the Anglo-Irish Corner family from the 1890's to the
1930's. Though the setting is mainly England and Ireland
(there are some African scenes in *Castle Corner*, however), the underlying theme of freedom as perpetual
creation or change and the war between incompatible
ideals is the same as in the African novel series. The continuity of the family itself with its symbolic "castle" was
to provide the unifying focus so that the seeming anarchy of events and warring ideas would be given order
and form.

Cary's early approach to the multiple novel form seems
to recapitulate the development of this literary genre.
Though on a much more limited scale, the African novel
series is similar to Balzac's *La Comèdie Humaine* with its

detailed exploration of all facets of a society and its use of an impersonal, detached narrator to achieve objectivity. The *Castle Corner* series is similar to Galsworthy's *Forsyte Saga*, using historical chronology and family history for continuity, and third-person narration for historical objectivity. These early attempts in the multiple novel constitute Cary's continuing search for a multiple view of reality. This search culminated in the development of the trilogy in which Cary realized a multiple view of realty through the interaction of narrator and form.

The Osborn Collection reveals that Cary originally conceived of the first trilogy as resembling a triptych with the middle "panel," *To Be a Pilgrim*, the major thematic focus of the whole. The three "voices" were to be a commentary on the others as well as themselves so that the whole would fold back on itself like a triptych. Cary had to modify this original plan because of the essential character of Sara, as he explains in the preface to *Herself Surprised*. He found he had to cut out some of the material on Sara in the other two novels because "there wasn't room for her." Though Cary modified the triptych idea in practice, the first trilogy is artistically successful as a multiple novel. It gives a truly multiple view of reality through the three distinct narrators; the style of each novel is distinct; and Cary develops an interlocking structure through theme and character so that the full meaning of any one of the novels is dependent on the other two.

Cary's first trilogy is artistically successful, and it is also a new development in the multiple novel: the three separate narrators, each with his own view of reality and his relationship with the other two narrators, represent a unique approach to the problem of form in the multiple novel. Arnold Bennett in his *Clayhanger* trilogy devoted the pattern of each novel to the development of one of the main characters, but the use of the omniscient third-person point of view results in a totally different perspective: instead of a multiple view of reality, we receive a single, over-all viewpoint. Cary's conception of human character in relation to reality was entirely different: "We are alone in our own worlds. . . . That's why each of my three chief characters had to write in the first person and reveal his own world in his own style." [3] Conrad made use of multiple narrators in a single novel, *Chance*, but the closest any multiple novel comes to Cary's narrative technique in the trilogies is Lawrence Durrell's *Alexandria Quartet*, with its use of multiple points of view and its multiple view of reality.

Cary's second trilogy more nearly resembles a triptych folding back on itself. The characters' lives are more closely bound together than in the first trilogy, and Nina Nimmo is a much more articulate "voice" than is Sara Monday; Nina's commentaries on Chester Nimmo and Jim Latter and on politics and history are more complex and sophisticated. The third "panel" of the triptych, *Not Honour More*, depends much more on its relationship to the first two novels than does *The Horse's Mouth*. Even so, *Except the Lord*, Nimmo's own story, is a modification of the triptych idea because it is concerned largely with Nimmo's early life, in which Nina played very little part and Jim Latter none at all. Nonetheless, *Except the Lord*, like *To Be a Pilgrim*, as the middle "panel" is the focus of the religious theme of the trilogy.

The Osborn Collection also reveals that Cary began to write another trilogy between the two published trilogies, experimenting with both first-person and third-person versions. One of the versions of this unpublished trilogy, which was to have the general title *The Captive and the Free* (a title Cary used for his last novel, though there is no similarity in material), is closely related to the Nimmo trilogy because the central situation involving Major Gye, his wife Kate, and Lord Drummer resembles the Nimmo-Nina-Latter triangle, and Major Gye is a prototype for Jim Latter in *Not Honour More*. Cary abandoned this trilogy, which is far from complete, to work on the

Chester Nimmo trilogy. It is evident that Cary used some of the material in the second trilogy from this incompleted trilogy. *Easy Money*, like *Prisoner of Grace*, is a defense of Lord Drummer from the point of view of a woman (Doatie Pilcher, his secretary and then wife); and *The Captive and the Free* volume, like *Not Honour More*, is a self-defense by Major Gye of his violent jealousy of Lord Drummer. However, probably because he wished to do a trilogy with politics at its center, Cary set aside *The Captive and the Free* to write the Nimmo trilogy.

Cary wanted to write a trilogy on each of what he felt to be the major creative activities of man—art, politics, and religion—and even before the completion of the second trilogy, he had a third one in mind. However, when in 1955 his fatal illness was diagnosed as muscular atrophy, he had to give up any plan to write the third trilogy. He used the remaining time of his life to work on the single novel *The Captive and the Free*, which was published posthumously in 1959. Though Cary was unable to fulfill his ambition to complete three trilogies, he did write on all three of man's creative activities, for *The Captive and the Free* treats of the artist of the soul, the religious spellbinder.

The form of the multiple novel used by Cary in the two trilogies is at the opposite extreme of narrative technique from the traditional omniscient point of view. It is important to realize that Cary (like Durrell) was not attempting to achieve a total view of reality simply by multiplying the points of view so that these different views would constitute the whole of reality. On the contrary, though each life touches on the others in interlocking relationships, what is ultimately suggested is that the human mind must be content with partial views of reality. Barbara Hardy suggests that Cary's plan for the first trilogy fails because when the main character of one novel becomes a minor character in the next, "he becomes an entirely different character." [4] Yet this is exactly Cary's intention: Sara as viewed by Gulley Jimson is quite a different person from Wilcher's Sara and from Sara's own view of herself, for paradoxically Sara in reality is all three Saras, different and contradictory, not just one of them, nor a single, transcendent synthesis of the three.

Other multiple novelists, such as Proust, C. P. Snow, and Anthony Powell, have avoided the metaphysical complexity of multiple narration by using the same narrator throughout their series. Cary and Durrell have sacrificed the values of continuity and control possible through a single point of view in order to achieve multiplicity. However, Durrell's notes appended to *Clea*, the last volume of the quartet, are not a confession of failure, but constitute a rationale for the multiple view of reality. Cary's modifications of the triptych theory are a recognition of the limitations imposed on him by the logic of his narrative material and method and not a denial of the multiple view of reality.

CHAPTER II

"THERE'S A WAR ON"
THE AFRICAN NOVELS

Aissa Saved
An American Visitor
The African Witch
Mister Johnson

AISSA SAVED (1932)

"*W*riting a book," Cary once commented, "is always an explanation as well as a setting forth. It is a spiritual structure in which one surveys a new part of one's world." [1] Among the manuscript versions of *Aissa Saved* there are at least six different beginnings. These rejected openings attest to Cary's method of constant revision:

I sketch a plan; I may write the end, the middle, and the beginning, and very often just in this order. That is, I decide how and where the book shall end, which is just as important to a book as a play; and then I ask myself where are the most difficult turns in the book. Then I may write one of these difficult passages to see if it is viable. And if, as often happens, it does not work, I may stop there. But if it does work, then I may devise a beginning and finish the book. [2]

Each scene or chapter as it is written may drastically affect and change what has already been written. This organic method is not limited to his early novels: Cary used it throughout his career. It is, he observed, "the only way in which I can get the kind of form I want, a certain balance and unity within a given context." [3]

Although the organic method explains in part why Cary revised constantly, much of his rewriting was based in a resourceful creative mind realizing more fully the potentiality of the material. For example, one of the early versions of the opening of *Aissa Saved* is as follows:

Mr. Cole [Carr], missioner of Shibi on the Niger, asked for volunteers to perform a dangerous service. It had come to his ears that the pagans of Kolu, on the other side of the river, were about to hold a rain-making feast, with the usual obscene rites; and his appeals to the District Officer to put a stop to practices useless and degrading, had been politely disallowed.

He was forced once more to the conclusion that nothing would be done to civilize Kolu, unless he did it himself.[4]

Later Cary saw the possibility of developing the Carrs as individualized characters by showing a conflict of attitude and purpose between them. He may have remembered or then written another version of the beginning which involves the refusal of the authorities to grant permission to the Carrs to open a branch of their mission in Yanrin:

Mr. Cole [Carr] was resigned to disappointment which he had expected, but Mrs. Cole [Carr] younger and more impatient, was very indignant that the conservatism and nervousness of the authorities should keep the knowledge of Christ's message from those who needed it the most.[5]

Carr's passive resignation and his wife's impatience are retained in the final version, but Cary may have seen more clearly the development of Carr as a character, for in the final version [6] Mrs. Carr's defiance of the authorities in landing a party of Christians at Kolu leads to a rediscovery of the emotional sources of his missionary zeal and to a reconciliation with his wife.

Another version of the opening exists in which Aissa, called Baju in this version, precipitates the action by going to Kolu:

Baju, a mission girl, got into trouble. She crossed the Niger into Kolu town where missions were forbidden and the pagans were excited against Christians, and struck on the nose MOSHALO, a priestess of the mountain-god. Then she ran for her life and being as light and quick as a deer escaped through dark alleys into the bush. She found her way by night to a place called KETENIFE where she persuaded a ferryman to smuggle her across the river.[7]

No doubt Cary at first sought to begin with some dramatic action taken by his protagonist, which would precipitate the war, but later he realized that the focus had to be first on Aissa's conversion to Christianity so that the internal conflict in Aissa's mind and the external conflict of the war would come to a climax simultaneously. Aissa is a much less zealous convert at the beginning than the mission girl of this version. Aissa's conversion has a practical and selfish basis: the mission is a refuge from the malicious gossip in Kolu that her baby is a witch and ought to be destroyed. Furthermore, her conversion is personal and emotional [8] not self-sacrificing, and the roots of her paganism are still very strong. Cary shows the development in Aissa of a sacrificial concept of Christianity which emerges from pagan as well as Christian origins so that in the end she sacrifices to Christ the baby she would not sacrifice to Oke the pagan god. It is a personal concept of sacrifice: she must sacrifice to Jesus that which she "like da mos."

Cary, in the draft of the letter addressed to his publisher, says that *Aissa Saved* is

an attack on one kind of sacrifice. It seeks to show that the idea of sacrifice, where removed from that of utility, of service, i.e. pleasing God, becomes pure juju and also self-indulgence. Thus Carr's conversion in the second [sic] chapter and Ojo's and Aissa's discovery in the last that to be happy it is only necessary to abandon personal responsibility and give up all to Christ are critical points. These are in fact surrenders—the escapes of human nature overpressed by responsibility of judgement.[9]

However, to assert that sacrifice not based on pleasing God is pure juju and self-indulgence begs the question of what pleases God. Carr's "conversion" in the fourth chapter can be said to be of service by bringing Christianity to the pagans even though it means defying man-made laws, and Ojo's and Aissa's discovery at the end was at least intended to help the cause of Christianity by bringing the rain that would convert the pagans. What Carr, Ojo, and Aissa have in common is not only a blind faith and trust in God by which they "abandon personal responsibility and give up all to Christ," but also the essence of Christian ethics, sacrifice of self as epitomized by the crucifixion. Aissa's offering of her child is from a rationalist's point of view a self-indulgent escape from personal responsibility, but both in the letter and in the printed preface Cary bases his judgment on Christian principles. And from a Christian point of view Aissa *is* saved; her sacrifice is as great an act of faith as the martyrdom of any Christian saint. Human sacrifice is a primitive pagan act of faith; Aissa's sacrifice is the obverse of Ishe's involuntary sacrifice of her son Numi to the pagan god Oke in a scene that parallels and foreshadows the end of the novel. Consciously or unconsciously, Cary has shown not that Christianity as brought to the Africans by the missionaries is merely a veneer adopted by native converts and superimposed on pagan beliefs and customs, but that Christianity itself with the symbolic sacrifice of Isaac and the actual sacrifice of Christ has its roots in primitive religions.

In the same manuscript draft of a letter to his publisher Cary states that *Aissa Saved* is not an attack on religion but is a study "of the effect of several kinds of education, atheist in Bradgate and Ali, materialist in Jacob, Christianity in the Carrs, Aissa, pagan in others, Mohammedan in the Emir." [10] Bradgate is the arch foe of the Carrs. His opposition to them is not on antireligious grounds, nor is he strictly speaking an atheist, but only a nominal Anglican who has not been to a church service for thirty years;

he has vague doubts about the Anglican creed, but he has never taken the time to look into his own beliefs. He opposes an extension of the Carrs' missionary work into Yanrin on the political grounds that it would excite an already restless people and on the economic grounds that the natives need a higher standard of living rather than education or enlightenment. Bradgate is essentially a rationalist seeking to conserve law and order in the region, but he is not motivated by "purely commercial and selfish" interests as Carr charges; with him it is a question of priorities, especially in the crisis over the drought. His motives, he suspects, are ethical, but he does not examine them because "he had no time to bother about such matters just now." [11]

In the preface to the Carfax edition of *Aissa Saved* Cary reveals that in revising the early versions he "cut out the religious philosophizing (chiefly between Bradgate and the Carrs) and rewrote the book several times in forms of increasing simplicity" (page 11). The following passage, canceled in a manuscript version, concerns Bradgate's reaction to Carr's letter:

> This letter was most effective in upsetting Bradgate's peace of mind and therefore annoying him; because it made him feel like an enemy of the light, one sunk in mean interests and narrow views. . . . He was in fact torn between two incompatable [sic] religions, the evangelical Christianity, learnt at his mother's knee, full of contempt for all such worldly qualities as critical judgement, intellectual integrity, curiosity, taste, tolerance, and that of a civilized European educated from sources far older, to esteem these among the highest virtues.[12]

In this version Bradgate is intellectually aware of the sources of his rationalism and of his vestigial doubts about his motivations. Cary, in making Aissa rather than Bradgate-Carr the focus of the novel's theme, deleted the abstract speculations. As a beginning novelist indebted to Hardy, Conrad, James, and the Russians, Cary was greatly tempted to keep the "Russian colloquy" and sacrifice what James called "the solidity of specification," but, he wrote, "as my own critic I rejected it" (page 11).

In another rejected passage Bradgate encourages the Carrs to go to Yanrin to pray for rain:

> I rather fancy rain is coming. The glass is down. It wouldn't do you any harm to have the credit of it.
>
> That's just what I say, Hilda exclaimed. Cole [Carr] did not know whether to be angry or to laugh. He laughed, and said You think it's a good chance.
>
> I want to see you make plenty of converts.
>
> It seems such a good chance to make these poor people know which is the true God, said Hilda.
>
> The two men looked at her; Bradgate charmed by the faith and simplicity; Cole [Carr] irritated by it.
>
> That's it, said Bradgate, thinking that he was saying the right thing. We're all in God's hands, aren't we. So I hope you'll do what you can for these poor lads.[13]

Bradgate leaves and the Carrs continue their argument, Hilda more certain they should go to Yanrin but Carr adamantly opposed to the scheme:

> Bradgate—he said with contempt and anger—don't you see that he looks upon witch doctors as little better than the local pagans. The typical British official. Without any more real religion in him than a boot. All in God's hand. Do you think he believes that. All in Man's hand, that's what he believes.[14]

In this version Bradgate is motivated by political expediency to favor the Christians over the witch doctors and by a personal cynicism to give the Carrs the benefit of his superior scientific knowledge. Carr recognizes that to accept Bradgate's offer would be to admit all is in man's hand, not God's, and that he would merely be taking advantage of the barometer reading. The logic of his position forces him to accept by implication the religious power of the witch doctors to make rain, for to deny it to them is to deny it to himself as God's missionary. The conflict of science and religion is brought to such a point that paradoxically Bradgate seems to be doing God's work, and Carr seems to be defending the witch doctors!

Cary probably rejected this version because it pin-pointed too neatly the conflict between science or ration-alism and religion, like an exercise book problem in logic. What matters, it is apparent in the published version, is not who makes the rain, but what violent emotions are released, what struggles for power and wars are waged, what injustices are done, what sacrifices are futilely made —all because of the conflict of differing ideas, educations, and religions, each separate proponent of which is posi-tive in the belief that his is the true and only way. This theme that each individual has of necessity only a partial view of reality underlies Cary's multiple point of view in the trilogies. Aissa, who makes the greatest sacrifice, does it solely for love of Jesus, not for the purpose of saving people or converting them to Christianity.[15]

Cary skillfully maintains an impersonal balance of forces among the warring ideas and the characters who are the embodiment of those ideas. Bradgate is right in warning that an attempt at this time by the Christians to preach to the pagans can only result in open conflict and disaster, as it does. But the sacrifice of Abba, Aissa's child, and the triumphant procession of the Christians across the river are the ironic counterpoints to the rationalist's view of the world, just as the ending of Huxley's *Point Counter Point* is an ironic counterpoint to Rampion's ra-tionalism. "Theirs is the kingdom of heaven" are Hux-ley's final ironic words as Beatrice and Burlap play like children in the bathtub; childlike, Ojo and Aissa weep and laugh together "kneeling beside Abba's body, crying out: 'Oh de joy, oh de joy, de joy of de Lord.' " "Theirs is the kingdom" is a title tentatively suggested by Cary for *Aissa Saved*, but eventually rejected.[16]

Cary's account in the final chapter of the ants eating Aissa alive is masterfully ironic. She attempts to fight off the ants, "crushing them by the hundreds. But they were soldier ants born and bred for self-sacrifice" (page 211). They sacrifice themselves "to get food for their community," as Aissa sacrificed her son for the good of the Christian community. Aissa's surrender to the ants leads to a vision of heaven. She holds out her arms to join Abba; she is overcome with joy; she is "helpless with laughter." The childlike innocence of Aissa is the apotheosis of self-sacrifice. Cary portrays equally the dramatic truth of Bradgate's worldly rationalism and Aissa's otherworldly Christianity. It is the ability to see "the fundamental injustice of the world" (page 9), and to see both sides of an issue impersonally, that is the key to Cary's ability to portray each character sympathetically no matter what side of the issue the character is on.

Ali, Cary tells us in the preface, was a young Nigerian who worked for him in his office at Kaiama (page 5). Originally Cary meant to make Ali the central character of this novel, contrasting "Ali's standards and ideas with those about him. This, of course, involved questions of local ethics, local religion, the whole conflict of those ideas in a primitive community; and also the impact of new ideas from outside" (pages 7–8). But, as the novel developed, Aissa "gradually became the heroine because she was more central to a deeper interest, that of religion" (page 8). Ali is only a minor character in the final version, but he is important because he represents the effect of education on the Nigerians and because he presents a contrast to both the pagans and the Christians. He is the Nigerian counterpart of Bradgate. Educated in the government school at Berua and assistant to the native treasurer Maaji Adamu, who can neither write nor add figures, Ali is highly conscious of his emancipated and superior ideas. He rescues Aissa and her child from being tried and condemned as witches, knowing from his education that justice is something administered by white judges, that rain is something that falls from clouds when they are cooled, and that witches have no power over rain.[17]

In the end it is Ali's education that defeats him. The Emir and his Mohammedan followers hate him for his superior airs. Jacob refuses to help him for the same reason: "You tink yourself better dan somebody" (page 174). The Christians, convinced he has betrayed them, kill him. Reduced to fear, he nonetheless prepares to die honorably: he "prepared himself to do the right thing and show the dignity and courage befitting a gentleman and a pupil of the Berua school" (page 193). He is cruelly beaten by the mob and loses his self-control before he dies, "but to the end he did not regret his bold enterprise" (page 193). He dies for his civilized belief that no one can make the rain. Ironically, his education is respected by the mob: "Many put pieces of flesh into their neck-bags for charms or philtres. For Ali had been a mallam. He could read and write and therefore he had magical powers" (pages 193–94).

In contrast, Jacob represents the worst adaptation of white civilization to native culture. He is, as Cary says, a materialist, who

valued himself as a man of the world whose axiom it is that all men and women, given the chance, are capable of any crime or vice. . . . His accomplishments which he fancied to be those of every white man were to drink raw whisky and gin without blinking, and to invent on the moment such lies and explanations as were calculated most surely to hide the defects and exaggerate the worth of any article the subject of bargaining. Jacob knew that it was contemptible in any man to hesitate at any trick or lie in the course of business [page 79].

His betrayal of Ali is motivated as much by the opportunity to show off in front of the crowd as it is by any dislike of Ali's superior ways.

The Emir, a Mohammedan, is at war with the Christians, but he is also against the new ideas of the white man's civilization. He is as much opposed to Bradgate's bridge-building and the increase of trade as he is to Ali's education:

Everything is getting worse, he would shout at them: "The clerks come, Yorubas, white men, these Christians now. All is being spoilt. . . . No railway, I say, no bridge—no roads, these are very bad things. Children must not go to school to learn to spit upon their mothers and fathers. We'll stop these Christians and their witchcraft" [pages 95–96].

But his opposition is ineffectual in stopping the progress of the white man's civilization or the strength of the Christians. Despite the Yanrin riots, MacEwen, the president of the court, backs up Bradgate's recommendation that more money be spent for education, roads, bridges, and markets, and two new Christian missions are set up in the area. The Christians become strong enough to declare a holy war, and they sack Kolu, and the Emir and his court are literally caught napping when the mob arrives. The Emir is a minor character in the novel, but he represents another aspect of the war between religions portrayed in the African novels.

As Cary's first novel, *Aissa Saved* is perhaps most interesting because it contains the seminal ideas of the other African novels; it explores the themes and characters that become the central focus of succeeding novels. Bradgate's rationalism is developed in Bewsher and Marie Hasluck of *An American Visitor*, and his belief in progress through roads and trade is portrayed in Rudbeck of *Mister Johnson*.[18] Mister Johnson is a larger life-sized portrait of Ali, and the Carrs become the Dobsons of *An American Visitor*. The Emir's ineffectuality is satirized in the doddering dying Emir of *The African Witch*, but the importance of the office itself is dramatized in the war between the forces of Louis Aladai and Salé. *An American Visitor* develops more explicitly the inevitability of the revolution taking place in Africa, *The African Witch* portrays more fully the racial conflict in colonial Africa, and *Mister Johnson* explores more complexly the effect of white civilization and education on the African mind. But all of these character types and themes, in greater or lesser degrees, are to be found in *Aissa Saved*. Although *Mister Johnson* is narrated in the present tense, the scenes describing Aissa's emotional re-

actions possess the same quality of the subjective immediacy of felt experience rather than being reported objectively by an impersonal observer. *Aissa Saved*, therefore, must be considered as the first novel of a series,
all of which "deal with this theme of war between incompatible ideals," rather than as an isolated first novel.
It is apparent that from the beginning Cary saw his material interrelatedly, and even the one novel of this early
period, *Castle Corner*, which is separate from the African novels, was planned as a trilogy.

AN AMERICAN VISITOR (1933)

In *An American Visitor* Joyce Cary turned to an examination of the white man's world in colonial Africa.
On the surface, it seems far different from *Aissa Saved*
in which the conflict of ideas wars in the mind and emotions of an African woman. And though the protagonists
of both novels are women, the contrast between them
seems as sharp and clear as the division between their
cultures, the one deeply rooted in primitive fears and
emotions, the other an emancipated white woman, a true
daughter of the enlightenment. *An American Visitor* is
different in its focus, but it is also closely related to *Aissa
Saved* as part of Cary's series on the war of cultures in
colonial Nigeria; the war is still on, but the point of view
has shifted to an exploration of the white man's culture in
Africa. Cary has chosen as his protagonist not an English-
man or Englishwoman committed to the colonial tradition, but an outsider, the American visitor Marie Hasluck, whose emancipated ideas are in conflict with English colonial policy.

In a letter to his publisher Cary explains the significance
of his use of the American woman:

Because her prejudices and ideals belong to America her
story is to some extent a commentary upon a fundamental

aspect of American civilization; but as the action takes place in a British dependency where Marie Hasluck falls in love with a British official and is involved therefore in the local politics, it raises also important and urgent questions about the policy and development of the Empire. . . .

The heroine of this book is described as a period piece; she doesn't know what she wants, but she wants it very badly. For Mr. Cary life is romantic in its essence; man feels before he thinks; and the quality of his emotions gives value to his character. But that quality depends chiefly upon the social & political & religious ideas of his period.

In this story of a modern American woman with the political & religious [ideas] of her time and country we see a passionate love-affair, a political theory and a religious creed as complementary expressions of the rare personality, the rare feeling about things, which is itself characteristic of a national sentiment.[19]

Although Cary here emphasizes Marie Hasluck's role as the embodiment of a national sentiment, in his retrospective prefatory essay written for the Carfax edition after he had visited America, he realized that Marie's "prejudices and ideals" were her own as an individual American rather than as a national type.[20] However, it is Marie as an outsider hostile to colonialism rather than her Americanism that is central to the novel's development: although intellectually opposed to the English colonial tradition, she becomes emotionally involved with it through her love for Bewsher. Her attempt to reconcile opposing ways of life through love ends in disaster. Cary's choice of a third-person narrator allows him to explore in an ironic detached manner another aspect of the war of incompatible ideals.

Andrew Wright suggests that *An American Visitor* is an uneven and unsatisfactory novel because Marie "is an idea rather than a human being." [21] This is a half-truth. Although Cary starts with the personification of a set of beliefs in the person of Marie Hasluck which is ridiculed by others, including Bewsher himself, he then humanizes her so that the clash between her beliefs and her personal

love results in tragedy. At the beginning of the novel
Marie is naïvely bound by her abstract generalizations of
life. She attributes to the Nigerians an ideal happiness un-
encumbered by the artificial social and religious institutions of Western civilization; they are to her Rousseau's
"noble savages" living in a state of natural happiness
which would be destroyed by adopting the white man's
laws and customs and Christian ethics. This Rousseauvian
view is implicitly ridiculed by the descriptions of the
Africans on the first page, long before it is expressed by
Marie some pages later.

Marie is uncompromisingly opposed to the missionaries
who would teach otherworldliness to the Africans, to the
miners who would bring the corrupting influence of the
white man's trade and commerce to the unspoiled region,
and at first to Bewsher himself because he would Euro-
peanize the Africans politically. For this Marie is held up
to ridicule by the colonial officials and the miners, and the
reader is prejudiced against her. Marie *is* naïve in her
idealism, but she is not ludicrous. Cary retains the role
of detached observer, for the ridicule heaped on Marie's
emancipated ideas reveals the narrowness of the colonialists: Jukes calls her a dangerous agitator, Allday accuses her of "teaching self-determination to bare-arsed
apes," and even the calm kindly Gore is shocked.

In the rejected versions of the beginning of this novel
Marie is more directly a personal object of ridicule. One
version begins as a letter to Gore the district officer:

The famous Hasluck—Mahrie Hasluck as she calls herself
—has caused more excitement in these parts than I can remember since the day when Lady Betty turned up at Gov-
vernment House in shorts. But that was ten years ago and
this woman isn't a beauty. She's rather like one of your own
pagans whitewashed or rather yellow washed, about four
foot high, with hair like old hay and little green eyes. She
went through here in a uniform like a boy scout's, but a good
deal dirtier than a boy scout ought to be. It's a slander to say
she doesn't wash. She does. All my carriers were privileged

to see her in her bath which she took coram publico. Her idea is that since the natives don't mind being looked at in their skins, why should she? [22]

Cary would have found it difficult to make such a person sufficiently attractive to Bewsher as well as the reader. In the published version the personal ridicule of Marie is relegated at the beginning to gossip among the Nigerians, who generalize her behavior as typifying white women. The criticism of Marie by the colonial officials and the miners is largely of her radical ideas about self-determination and the need to preserve the African customs and way of life.

The crux of the novel, on which its meaning and achievement depends, is the development of Marie Hasluck's character from this personified idea to the point where, having found herself through love for Bewsher, she becomes the tragic victim of her own ideals. After finding personal happiness and love in her marriage, she "comes to believe that God is the god of love—out of her love for Bewsher." She is a prisoner of her own habit of mind: "She wants a world without grief and sorrow, pain, injustice and despair, and she knows she can't have it, at first." [23] In the crisis at the end of the novel she does not want to choose between a selfish protection of Bewsher and an acceptance of disillusionment about her ideals: "she felt in her breast an intolerable longing—she wanted to cry—for the silly young woman who had seen in a little community of naked savages the pattern of an earthly paradise" (page 193).

Marie is converted to the idea that God is love by the missionary Dobson. Her idealism needs but an act of faith to prove itself, and it is Dobson who provides the previously skeptical Marie with the idea for the act of faith: "love is stronger than guns," he tells her. [24] Convinced that she can have the best of two worlds, the real world of her love for Bewsher and the ideal world of justice and love and friendship, she hides the gun that might

save her husband's life, so sure is she that the natives will
not kill Bewsher who is their friend. But in the war between the whites and the Africans, Bewsher is wrongly
blamed by the Africans for allowing the miners to extend
their operation. Marie's act of faith is a futile gesture,
and Bewsher's death is the result.

Bewsher himself has no illusions about the danger involved; he knows he rules by force of prestige and would
have used the gun to save himself. Bewsher, as he dies,
sees it as a turn of bad luck: "Well, old chap, the joke
is on you. You're not going to get away with it this time"
(page 229). Both Bewsher and Marie are victims of the
tragic irony that events have outmoded the concept of
their roles in Africa. Bewsher gravely underestimates the
violent hatred of the Africans toward him which overcomes their fear of his prestige. It is Cottee the prospec-
tor, whom both the Africans and Bewsher oppose, who
wins out, for he represents the inevitable revolution taking place in Africa. Marie gravely overestimates Bewsher's power of persuasion which events have made im-
potent. Ironically, her act of faith provides Obai with
the chance to achieve happiness by reaching "his crown
of glory" in killing Bewsher.[25]

Marie comes to realize that personal love and happiness
can be destroyed by the injustice of this unideal world.
She learns too late that "if no one was to die or suffer
there wouldn't be any love, and if no one was to get
killed there wouldn't be any life worth living" (page
237). Bewsher understood all along, as Cary notes: *"It is
necessary to suffer to be happy."*[26] But Marie understands
this only after Bewsher is killed; she believed there could
be no conflict between her own happiness and her idealistic desire to see everyone else happy.

Unlike Aissa, Marie is not "saved" but she is humanized
by her suffering and remorse; where Aissa is "sanctified"
by her sacrifice, Marie is made compassionate and hum-
ble. The reader comes to sympathize with her, and when
she kneels at Bewsher's grave and says, "I'm not praying,

but where [Bewsher] is, the ground feels kind of different" (page 239), the reader is moved by the power of her love at the same time he understands the force of the idealism that motivated her.

An American Visitor develops the theme of love and sacrifice explored in *Aissa Saved*. Marie's act of faith, when examined closely, is the obverse of Aissa's. Aissa sacrifices her child and herself for love of Jesus; Marie, unknowingly and involuntarily, sacrifices Bewsher to the concept that God is love. In an earlier version of the crucial scene Marie does not hide the pistol but takes out the magazine and gives the gun to Bewsher unloaded; she does it because, as she says to Bewsher, "You won't change now after all the years when you've never used violence. Don't you see that you're safer when you go as a friend when God's spirit is with you." [27] Though these words are not used in the published version, they are implicit in the situation. Marie's sacrifice is as futile as Aissa's, but it arises from the same impulse of faith. Both Marie and Aissa are victims of events beyond their control.

What prevents Marie and Bewsher from being tragic figures at the end is that they are seen from the point of view of Cottee. For a moment Cottee is moved by the compassionate figure of Marie at Bewsher's grave and is transported by the scene "into another state of being, where men and women were born to heroic destinies, and life was the magnificent stage of their glories and their suffering" (page 238). But "this fit of poetical fervour" dissolved "like a transformation scene," and Cottee thinks, "This ugly little woman a tragic queen, Monkey Bewsher a hero, it was absurd" (page 238). Cary did not want to romanticize Marie and Bewsher, and Cottee's analysis serves the same function as Marlow's analysis of Lord Jim in Conrad's novel.

It would be a mistake, however, to view Cottee as Cary's spokesman. Cottee is no Conradian narrator analyzing the romantic temperament from the security of a rational code of conduct. As the representative of the new civilization, he is as vulnerable as Bewsher, who attempts to oppose the revolution, and Gore, who hopes to make peace between the two factions but who must eventually give in to change. Cottee rides the tide of change and thus wins over Bewsher. He triumphs (and profits) because the revolution triumphs: "how could any man hope to fight against it when it came with the whole drive of the world behind it . . . ?" (page 234). His cynicism is revealed in his pity for men like Bewsher and Gore: "man only had one life and if he wanted to enjoy it he had better suit his taste to his times and not try to change the times to suit his taste" (page 236). Although he foresees a new civilization evolving out of the ruins of the old with new values and new standards that "might take forms more austere and rigid than anything known to them" (page 236), Cottee cannot see the point to the Russian story of the old lady who tried to save her beautiful cabinets and china and thus assured their being destroyed by the revolutionary soldiers. To him she is holding to outmoded values; the cabinets and the china are replaceable. He cannot understand that these particular objects are unique, are irreplaceable, no matter how many new things are made and created. He cannot understand the irony of the woman's attempt to save her beautiful things by appealing to the soldiers' nonexistent finer instincts—"What did she expect?" is his comment.

Cary has achieved a balance of forces among the various points of view in the clash of ideas. His is a Huxleyian detachment (the early Huxley, that is) rather than a Conradian commitment. It enables him to realize both the absurdity and the idealism of Marie's faith, the anachronism and the romantic heroism of Bewsher's devotion to the Birri's cause, the ineffectuality and the humaneness of Gore's middle-of-the-road policy, and the vulgarity and the truth of Cottee's revolution. It is this ability to see all sides that enables Cary to explore the complex war of ideas and cultures with sympathetic detachment.

It is Cary's ability to portray contradictory ideas and

views objectively and convincingly that Robert Bloom calls Cary's "indeterminateness," an "intellectual irresolution" that deprives his novels of a moral center.[28] I believe it is more understanding of Cary's multiple view of reality to suggest that this empathic ability to submerge his own view of reality is related to Keats' idea of the negative capability: "A poet is the most unpoetical of anything in existence, because he has no Identity—he is continually in for and filling some other body." Thus, Cary portrays sympathetically the views of both the primitive Aissa and the emancipated Marie Hasluck, the evangelistic Carrs and the rationalistic Bradgate, the romantic Bewsher and the materialistic Cottee. And in *The African Witch* he presents convincingly all sides of the racial and religious conflict. Cary's "neutrality" in the war of ideas is not intellectual irresolution but is the objective detachment necessary in the novel of ideas with its contrapuntal technique of contrasting ideas and attitudes in dramatic conflict with each other.

THE AFRICAN WITCH (1936)

In the prefatory essay to the Carfax edition of *The African Witch* Cary wrote, "This book began in a sketch, made sometime in the middle twenties, of an African nationalist. I called him the Black Prince, and he was, as far as I can remember, a much more violent and hysterical man than Aladai." [29] One of Cary's early unpublished works, entitled *Aladé*, [30] is more explicitly concerned with the theme of African nationalism than is *The African Witch*. [31] Aladé, whether or not he is the Black Prince of the sketch, is more closely related to the "violent and hysterical man" Cary mentions than he is to the sophisticated Oxford-educated Louis Aladai of *The African Witch*. Louis Aladai's anger is a cold controlled fury when, having been insulted and struck by Rackham, he says to his sister Elizabeth, the ju-ju priestess, "I am a Rimi man. Take these clothes away and burn them" (page 210). But the protagonist of *Aladé*

> tore his clothes to pieces and trampled on them screaming at the startled deputation in Husa. See then, these are white and I wish they were all the whites together so that I could smash them into porridge. What are you afraid that I'll go with the whites, those foul beasts, those liars and cowards, after what they did to me. You say they were my friends. I know them better than you do, and I tell you I'd rather cut off my hands than touch their lepers skin—As usual when he began to speak of his wrongs, he lost control of himself, his words became obscene violenent [sic]; he could not find any words [foul] and ugly enough to express his hatred; he screamed and danced on the torn trousers foaming at the mouth.[32]

This passage is important for what it reveals of Cary's changing concept of his main character. In the early work Aladé's Europeanization goes no deeper than the clothes he wears; it is a veneer thinly hiding his essential primitive nature. In *The African Witch* Aladai's European clothes symbolize part of his nature because he *is* Europeanized; and that part of him is in conflict with his own people, represented by his pagan sister, and with the whites who do not accept him as an equal even though he is more intelligent and better educated than most of them. Thus Cary has portrayed a three-dimensional character in Louis Aladai whose education and intelligence is in tragic conflict with his background, his race, his aspirations, and with events. Aladé is a less complex character who, like Aissa, is governed largely by his emotions and by his primitivism.

Aladé's hysterical violence weakens a corollary theme in the early version—the racial prejudice of the white men and women. The description of Aladé screaming and foaming at the mouth mitigates in part the racist views of the colonialists. But in *The African Witch* Louis Aladai is a civilized and intelligent man, the intellectual equal and even superior of the colonial officials and their wives, and the contempt of the whites magnifies the stupidity of racial prejudices. Louis Aladai, like E. M. Forster's Dr. Aziz in *Passage to India*, is the victim of his own emancipation, for an English education will free his mind but it will not change the color of his skin.

The beginning of *Aladé* is remarkably similar to *The African Witch*, even though the characters' names are different:

An extraordinary incident took place at Pawu Races. Pawu is in an accessible point on the Dirina river in Northern Nigeria and its races are attended by great crowds of natives and white people from considerable distances. Sometimes there are thirty or forty white men and a dozen women. These of course have their own enclosure from which the natives except the Emir and his chief officers, and a few servants, are excluded.

But on this occasion, just after the first race, when the spectators turned from the rope marking the edge of the course, it was seen that a native had entered the enclosure, a tall very black young man dressed in white ducks and wearing a white helmet. It was still more surprising to see him in animated conversation with the Residents niece, a girl called Nancy Nolle. There they stood apparently totally unaware of the sensation they were causing. The girl was turning up her eyes toward the tall black man, blushing and smiling, with a look of the most flattered delight and the other bending over her in an easy and gallant pose, was talking rapidly, waving his hands, shrugging his big shoulders, laughing so that his white teeth could be seen glittering twenty yards away, like a new moon. As a disgusted soldier (it was Scott) put it, she might have been a flapper making the acquaintance of her Gerald or her Owen, and he added "But I can't understand whats bitten her. Where's Pole. Why doesn't he stop it."

Captain Pole was chairman of the race committee, starting handicapper etc. and seemed to be the right person to drive out the intruder and rescue Miss Nolle. But Pole was saying at the same time "Look at that ape—what in God's name does he think he's playing at." [33]

If one substitutes the names Judy Coote for Miss Nolle
and Captain Rackham for Captain Pole, the similarity
between the two beginnings is striking; but there is an
important difference. The third-person narrator of the
early version is by the choice and tone of his words indignant at the intrusion; he is by implication committed
to racist attitudes (this is evident also in the passage describing Aladé's hysterical anger). The narrator of the
published version, while also a white man, is a detached
observer reporting the incident objectively. This objectivity is essential to Cary's role as impersonal author and
historian of the war of cultures. As he writes in his preface
to *The African Witch*, each side "is trying to persuade
the other (as well as himself) that his creed is the only
reasonable truth, and that outside it there is in fact nothing
but darkness and devils" (page 10). Africa is the chosen
setting because "it shows these wars of belief, and the
powerful often subconscious motives which underlie
them, in the greatest variety and also in very simple
forms. Basic obsessions, which in Europe hide themselves
under all sorts of decorous scientific or theological or political uniforms, are there seen naked in bold and dramatic
action" (page 10). Thus *The African Witch* continues
the series, "There's a War On," and more than any other
of the African novels it describes a war between the races.

Cary denies in his preface that his novel is an attack on
colonial administration, a work about the color bar, or a
tract on the need for education. Certainly, to view the
book solely from one viewpoint is to oversimplify the
problems involved. If Cary as a writer has the quality of
negative capability, he has also as a thinker the quality of
seeing all sides of an issue, a virtue of the liberal imagination, which enables Cary (like Huxley in his early
novels) to dramatize warring ideas, convincingly presenting opposite views in order to achieve the necessary
dramatic balance between conflicting ideas.

On the racial issue the colonialists condemn themselves
by their words and actions. As in Forster's *Passage to India*

it is the wives rather than the officials who are the more outspoken and vehement. Mrs. Pratt is nearly hysterical over the opening incident: "They ought to be put down and beaten. That's the only way to teach such brutes!" (page 15). And Dryas Honeywood, though much less vehement in her emotions, agrees with Mrs. Pratt's attitude: "I do hate people like that—they're so frightfully pushing, that kind of black man" (page 16). Miss Honeywood, however, is a newcomer to Africa and not so emotionally committed to racism. She later befriends Louis Aladai, not because she has become emancipated but because she wants to avoid trouble; Aladai presumes a friendship and an equality with her because she does not snub him. Yet it is Dryas Honeywood who, like Adela Quested in *Passage to India*, precipitates the critical incident in which Captain Rackham strikes Aladai and knocks him into the river. But it is Judy Coote who more closely resembles Adela Quested in actively seeking out Aladai and professing friendship for him.

If Dryas Honeywood and Judy Coote are complementary aspects of Forster's Adela Quested, then Captain Rackham and Honeywood in their racial prejudices are complementary aspects of Forster's Ronny Heaslop. I do not intend to suggest that Cary modeled his novel on Forster's *Passage to India* or that he was necessarily influenced by Forster. The two novels are essentially different, but a comparison is rewarding in that both novels reveal the repetitive pattern of racial attitudes and incidents and the similar types of mentality and motivation among the racially prejudiced.

Louis Aladai and his sister Elizabeth are the two major African characters in *The African Witch*. Though she is not as complex and fully developed a character as her brother, Elizabeth Aladai is as important as he to the final meaning of the novel. She represents the Rimi civilization from which Louis has been freed by his Oxford education. In the beginning Louis is contemptuous of Rimi civilization and wholly admiring of European civilization

with which his aspirations are identified. He says to Judy
Coote:

> "Rimi civilization! You know that it is a joke. Can you
> compare it with yours?—and that means all Europe. Think
> of the richness of the European peoples—the poetry, the
> music . . . the greatness of every kind." He turned on her
> again. "Rimi civilization! Do you know what it is?—*ju-ju*"
> [page 24].

Louis is emancipated intellectually from his primitive
origins. But Elizabeth is his sister, symbolically suggesting
(and later embodying) that part of him which emotionally and psychologically he cannot escape. He is driven
by events and his own aspirations to take off his European
clothes and wear Rimi clothes.

From the very beginning Louis, because of his political
aspirations, compromises his intellectual emancipation by
tolerating the evangelical emotionalism of Coker; though
he is contemptuous of Coker's "primitive religious *ju-ju*"
he accepts his support, certain that he can stop him any
time. (This necessity for expediency in the power struggle
of politics foreshadows the destruction of his identification with European civilization.) He cannot control
Coker's violence any more than he can control his body's
reaction to Coker's ju-ju, the decapitated head of Doctor
Schlemm.

Though he may talk on familiar and equal terms with
the idealistic Judy Coote and even dance with the con-
science-ridden Dryas Honeywood, no number of Oxford
degrees could make Louis acceptable to the white community. His pathetic attempt to achieve acceptance by
the whites at their club is followed by the inevitable
snub as he quotes Wordsworth. What might be acceptable in an Oxford drawing room will not do at the Scotch
club in Nigeria; Scotch and Wordsworth do not mix.

Louis Aladai's aspirations are doomed from the start
because his education does not free his body from the
color of his skin. Yet it is not foolish pride or selfish

ambition that motivates him. He *is* the intellectual equal (and better) of the whites; he *does* have a valid claim to the Emir's throne from which he would rule half a million people; and if he is motivated by a sense of personal destiny and greatness, it is because he, as he reminds himself, has been the one chosen to receive an education so as to be able to lead his people.

It is Elizabeth Aladai who triumphs in the end. Disillusioned with his adopted civilization and betrayed by the whites, Louis strips himself of his European nature and joins forces with Elizabeth and Coker against his rival, the Mohammedan Salé who, by murdering the old Emir, has installed himself as Emir with the tacit acceptance of the Resident, Burwash. The war which ensues is a futile one and both Aladai and Coker are killed by white troops; only Elizabeth, in the women's war, is successful, and ironically is praised for her moderation in the official report. The result, symbolized by Elizabeth's triumph over Akande Tom, is not only a personal defeat for Louis Aladai but an end to his dreams of an advanced civilization for Rimi. In an ironic parody of the Christian parable of the triumph of good over evil, Elizabeth makes Tom crawl to her on his hands and knees like a snake, not merely as a gesture of domination over the man but more significantly as the triumph of her pagan ju-ju over the white man's ju-ju, education. Tom's will is crushed. The English play tennis and polo and drink tea as before. Colonial life and manners remain unchanged; only Judy Coote is left to voice the conscience of a race, and she loses Tom to Elizabeth.[34]

The African Witch is the most complex and complicated of Cary's African novels, combining many elements of theme and character that are treated separately in the other novels. The practice of ju-ju and witchcraft is revealed even more extensively than in *Aissa Saved*, where it is a major part of the plot. As one of the many interrelated threads in the narrative pattern of this novel, the story of Ibu, the girl who is accused of being a witch, is woven in and out of the main plot. Hers is the terror of one helplessly caught in a web of circumstances not merely beyond her control but beyond her understanding; this is reflected and intensified by the more articulate and rational Osi who is also accused of being a witch. The terrible power over life and death that resides in the ju-ju priestess, Elizabeth Aladai, is real; she believes in her own magic, and the people themselves believe in it (page 33). Ibu escapes, or rather she is pushed out of the ju-ju house by Osi who wants to escape; ironically, Ibu wants to escape because she is convinced Osi is a witch and means to kill her. But freedom is frightening to her; the world into which she escapes is as frightening as the ju-ju house. In her wanderings she first attaches herself to a gang of young boys who in their games parody the antics of their elders, and then to Fanta, one of the Emir's women; but when Salé murders the old Emir and installs himself in the palace as Emir, Ibu is captured by Elizabeth. Inexorably, as though the pattern of events are fated, Ibu finds herself once more in the ju-ju house, but her escape is taken as a sign that she has strong magic powers, and Elizabeth adopts her and prepares her for priesthood as though she had been destined all along to be a ju-ju priestess.

The doddering senile Emir seems a parody of the Emir in *Aissa Saved,* and the dignity of his words is destroyed by his ludicrous walk, the ineffectual attempts to assert authority, the great gulf between the ceremonial dignity of his office and the actual indignity of his person. There seems to be a suggestion here that the great struggle for power between Aladai and Salé is an empty one, as empty as the ceremonial powers of the Emirate, for the real power resides in the white colonial officials, and though they invite the Emir and his ministers into their paddock at the races, they do not talk to them. "They were an ornament to the occasion" (page 15).

Coker and Doctor Schlemm represent opposite poles of Christian action. Coker, with his militant evangelism and

his violent "*ju-ju* of blood," is a foil to Doctor Schlemm's
Christian humanitarianism and Louis Aladai's faith in the
emancipating power of education. It is not an accident of
plot that Coker kills and decapitates Schlemm: it is the
tragic outcome of the dichotomy in Christian beliefs, the
one leading to violent sacrifice of blood to rid the world
of evil (Aissa is "saved"), the other leading to humani-
tarian impulses based on an ideal concept of love (Marie
Hasluck's God is love). As Cary states in an unpublished
note, "Schlemm has grasped fact. Life's spring is emotional. [Its] Driving force—love [—] won't solve problems but it may give will to solve them and direction to
solution." [35] As a rational Christian, Doctor Schlemm is
the determined foe of ju-ju and witch doctors, and as a
clergyman he is the opposite of Coker, whom he considers "the worst enemy of Christianity." That the two clash
is inevitable, but that Coker defeats Schlemm does not
suggest that Cary believes the violent blood-hate kind of
Christianity is most dominant, only that in Africa it can
lead to savage conflict. Ironically, Schlemm, the enemy
of ju-ju, becomes Coker's powerful ju-ju which converts
Louis Aladai involuntarily to violence.

Captain Rackham, besides representing the general
attitude of the white colonial officials towards the natives,
precipitates Louis Aladai's crisis of divided loyalties by
striking him. It would be an oversimplification of the complex theme of this novel to see Rackham's action as totally a racist incident, which in part it is. Rackham is also
a victim of events not of his own making. Caught between
the two women he loves, Judy Coote and Dryas Honeywood, he is driven to an action which overcomes his usual
aloofness. He is not indignant with Judy for talking to
Louis Aladai in the opening incident, nor is he moved to
violence toward Aladai; he is indignant "with something
else, larger and vaguer—fate perhaps" that should involve
him in an incident. He did not at first deliberately intend to snub Aladai at the Scotch club, but in the end he
does it impulsively, in exasperation. Events force Rack-

ham and Aladai into being personal enemies; Judy Coote,
an English version of Marie Hasluck, had known Louis
Aladai at Oxford long before she met Rackham, and her
emancipated views enable her to accept Louis Aladai as a
friend; Dryas Honeywood, with whom Rackham falls in
love though he is engaged to Judy, befriends Louis
Aladai not because she likes him—in actuality she is
prejudiced—but because she feels she "ought to" like
Negroes. Rackham has no more control over these
situations than he does over his passions which make him
fall in love first with the one girl and then the other and
finally cause him to strike Louis Aladai in exasperation.

All of these interrelated stories and themes form an
intricate pattern in the novel, presenting a complex but
integrated picture of the war of beliefs. Cary did not
experiment in style in this novel as he does in *Mister
Johnson;* stylistically *The African Witch* is similar to the
first two novels, using the impersonal, objective, detached
tone of the third-person observer and reporter of *Aissa
Saved* and *An American Visitor*. What is experimental is
the contrapuntal technique of relating and controlling
several threads of narration at once and weaving them
into a complex whole. Both *Aissa Saved* and *An American Visitor* utilize this technique to some extent, but in
The African Witch it becomes the dominant narrative
pattern of the novel. It is a technique which Cary uses
even more extensively in his next published novel, *Castle
Corner*.

MISTER JOHNSON (1939)

Professor Mark Schorer, reviewing *Mister Johnson* in
the *New York Times*, says that Cary portrays the "immediacy of experience that the most distinguished novelists of the 20th century have come to regard as of secondary importance," attributing this in part to the effect of
the present-tense style which his "rapid yet narrative

effects often show." [36] In his preface to the Carfax edition Cary defends his use of the present tense: "it was chosen because Johnson lives in the present, from hour to hour . . . as Johnson does not judge, so I did not want the reader to judge. And as Johnson swims gaily on the surface of life, so I wanted the reader to swim, as all of us swim, with more or less courage and skill, for our lives." [37] Cary does not use the present tense as part of a stream of consciousness technique. The reflective thoughts of his protagonist are unknown. But then Mister Johnson is no Stephen Dedalus or Clarissa Dalloway; he is not even a Louis Aladai reflecting with a European mind while he reacts to the immediacy of Coker's ju-ju; nor a Tabitha Baskett, the protagonist of *A Fearful Joy*, reflecting the history both personal and national of the first half of the twentieth century while living it in the present tense. Mister Johnson is himself, the poet of the moment.

A discarded opening scene of *Mister Johnson*, written in the past tense, shows why Cary ultimately selected the present tense for this novel:

There was a row in the divisional office. Old Brook had caught one of the clerks in some petty swindle. His loud contemptuous voice came through the door; obviously he was too disgusted to be angry.

"You understand that its a criminal charge—the penalty is up to five years—what have you to say?"

There was a faint mutter.

"Very well—where is the money why weren't the wood-men paid."

Another faint mutter.

Rudbeck, waiting on the stoop to see the resident, mused to himself at the crushing politeness of old Brook's voice. How Brook did hate clerks. The three messengers showed no interest whatever.[38]

Johnson is finally told by Brook to leave:

The clerk came out. He was a thin coffee-coloured boy with large black eyes and rather small neat features; a straight nose, a mouth curved in classical style. . . .

Rudbeck said in surprise "Why its Mr. Johnson." The clerk turned and at once his look changed to one of astonishment and delight. He stooped as if about to fall at the young man's feet and said "Oh sir, I prayed God for you—"

Rudbeck was taken aback. He was a young official in his first term and he had only met Johnson once before, three months ago, for five minutes, in another office. . . . His exclamation had been mainly surprise.[39]

In the above version the reader is removed from the moment of experience by the historical perspective; he remains at a critical distance from Mister Johnson. In the final version the narrator is present at the moment of experience; the reader is drawn into the current of events by the illusion of being present when things happen; he is closer to Johnson because he shares with him the feelings of the moment. This is best illustrated by comparing the passage in the novel which most nearly parallels the original version:

The very look of him [Rudbeck] now on the stoop gives him [Johnson] such a shock of joy and relief that he bursts into tears. Johnson, after all, is only seventeen and completely alone. He falters, "Oh, Mister Rudbeck, may God bless you—I pray for you all time."

Rudbeck, not very good at distinguishing one black face from another, or remembering them, stares at the boy from under his shelving forehead and says, "Hullo-hullo. What's the trouble? Why, it's thingummy-tite, aren't you?" [page 23].

The use of the present tense gains the reader's involvement in the immediate experience without any real sacrifice of the narrator's detachment as an observer. The reader's emotions are engaged, and at the same time he is made aware that Johnson's "friendship" with Rudbeck exists only in Johnson's mind as a romantic illusion.

Mister Johnson begins with Johnson falling in love at first sight with Bamu, the ferryman's daughter. From that point Johnson's life is turned into a romance. He tells Bamu "that he is a government clerk, rich and powerful.

He will make her a great lady" (page 11), a civilized lady who will wear white women's dresses and sit in a chair and eat with him. Mister Johnson is in love with Bamu, but he is also in love with his dream: he will have a white man's wedding, not the primitive ceremony (they have both); he will present Bamu to Rudbeck's wife and they will be friends (Bamu refuses to wear the dress he has bought her and appears in her native cloth; Bamu and Celia Rudbeck remain as separate as their symbolic costumes). The reader is aware from the beginning that Johnson's dreams of glory are a figment of his active imagination, and if there is any doubt the narrator dissolves it by matter-of-factly reporting that Johnson's idea of a civilized marriage is gleaned from store catalogues, fashion notes, observations of missionaries, and some approved novels, "a compound of romantic sentiment and embroidered underclothes" (page 13). The reader learns also that "Johnson is a temporary clerk, still on probation, called up on emergency from a mission school. He has been in Fada six months and is already much in debt" (page 16), giving grand parties commensurate with his sense of importance.

Why is it then that the reader is carried along with Johnson on the "surface of life"; why is it that Johnson is wholly accepted and even admired by the reader and not dismissed as an egoist, a liar, and a thief? Part of the answer, as has been indicated, is Cary's use of the present tense which, coupled with the lack of chapter divisions, sweeps the reader along in the current of events. But also part of the answer is Cary's portrayal of Johnson as "a poet who creates for himself a glorious destiny" (page 5); Johnson's imaginative sense of life as a romance creates the illusion of life as a comedy, an illusion which the reader accepts because of Johnson's exuberant love of life and infectious laughter and songs. Having been caught up in the romance of Johnson's "glorious destiny," the reader shares the shattering of that illusion. The comic mask of life is ripped off, revealing not a face but another mask, the tragic mask that lies beneath comedy. The reader, like Rudbeck, is trapped by his own illusions.

Rudbeck, the district officer for whom Johnson works, is central to our understanding of Johnson's tragedy. He is Cary's best portrait of the colonial official in the African novels. He combines the road-building mania of Bradgate in *Aissa Saved* and the idealism of Bewsher in *An American Visitor*, but unlike Bradgate and Bewsher who are not personally involved with the lives of the African characters, Rudbeck is a central figure in the novel because of his personal relationship with Johnson. Paradoxically, at the beginning, the great gulf between Johnson the native and Rudbeck the white man is emphasized to show the false illusion on which Johnson's dream is built; Johnson brags that Rudbeck is his great friend, but Rudbeck does not even remember his name when they meet again. Ordinary politeness to an underling is interpreted by Johnson as positive evidence of friendship. Yet Rudbeck is affected and amused by the poetry of Johnson's mind that causes him to file a report on nonexistent native tobacco under elephant poachers because Rudbeck had once told him that the tobacco was green like elephant droppings.

Without Johnson, Rudbeck would never have completed his road; without being a poet like Johnson, Rudbeck would never have begun his road. The road, which is the creative expression of his imagination as much as any of Johnson's schemes, reveals the close relationship between the two men. Johnson, with his self-imagined sense of glorious destiny, is the alter-ego of Rudbeck, with his vision of glory as master road-builder. While building the road Rudbeck is happy and fulfilled, but when the road is finished and the great idea is realized he "feels as if life holds nothing more for him" (page 165). The building of the road symbolizes the creative imagination at work, realizing itself as an end in itself, but when the road is completed reality takes over. Civilization takes over the road and brings with it an increase in trade and crime and the destruction of old ways for which Rudbeck is blamed. The road is the direct symbol of the revolution taking place in Africa: "I am the revolution," it says. Rudbeck is confused and frustrated by its meaning; he feels "he has been used and driven like a blind instrument" (page 169).

Johnson suggests the practical means by which Rudbeck can realize his goal of completing the road—"borrowing" on next year's road fund or, as Rudbeck puts it to himself more bluntly, "stealing from my own Treasury." If it is Johnson who suggests, it is Rudbeck who acts; and if Johnson knows how to juggle the accounts, he has learned this from the whites. Rudbeck's embezzlement is discovered by Tring, who temporarily takes over while Rudbeck goes on leave. Rudbeck is found out because Johnson in the best approved white man's tradition has kept careful accounts of all the falsified vouchers by which the material and labor for the road were paid out of other funds so that Tring has direct evidence of Rudbeck's manipulation of the funds.

Significantly, Johnson's downfall closely follows the completion of the road and Rudbeck's disillusionment. The deeper Rudbeck commits himself to the road and the harder he works, the faster the road is completed, ending the happiness its creation gave him. Similarly, the more Johnson gets into debt, the deeper he commits himself to his hollow dream of power and glory by wild schemes and desperate actions, bringing about the inevitable crisis which destroys him. He is deserted by his wife, but we know all along that she will desert him the moment his fortunes decline, as surely as we know Johnson will be destroyed by his romanticism, for Bamu's love exists only in his imagination and is part of the imagined paradise that is destroyed by reality. He is betrayed by his friends, but we know all along that Ajali and Waziri are not really his friends and will betray him when expedient to do so, for their friendship exists only in his imagination. Johnson himself disintegrates as his world crumbles about him; his behavior becomes more wild and savage and his actions more desperately criminal. He is no longer comic as he prepares to rob Gollup in a last desperate action to save his dream. Gollup catches him, and Johnson murders him.

Sarje Gollup, the owner of the store where Johnson once worked, is a foil to Rudbeck. He is a violent, irrational man, a racist, a trader who cheats his customers more than Johnson cheats him; he is a realist in contrast to Rudbeck. As a man of commerce and trade he will benefit from the new road while Rudbeck is blamed for the crime wave. His being killed by Johnson is accidental rather than inevitable except in the sense that he is killed protecting what he values most, his money. What is inevitable about his murder is that Johnson's romanticism leads him to this final catastrophe.[40]

It is Rudbeck who, as sheriff, magistrate, and coroner, must arrest, judge, and dispose of Johnson. In an early manuscript version, Cary concludes the novel with Rudbeck executing Johnson by his own hand, but the emphasis during the trial scene and the execution is significantly different from the published text. The focus in the original version is on Rudbeck rather than on Johnson:

All at once, Rudbeck is aware of himself and Johnson, as they really are. He sees them isolated and real in the silence. He sees himself sitting in his chair, in his best uniform, with his hair brushed, calm aloof and official, in the attitude of a mock official devotion. He feels with overwhelming force Johnson's living reality; his agony, his courage.

He feels mean and contemptible, his correct attitude, his sympathy appear a technique used to protect him from the need of real action, real responsibility.[41]

In the published version Cary has rightly shifted the narrative focus to Johnson, for as long as Johnson is alive he is the central focus of the novel. Both versions end with Rudbeck, partly as a justification and partly as a plea for understanding, explaining he had to execute Johnson himself.

Johnson is guilty of murder; of that there is no doubt. He has killed a white man, and since he is being judged under white man's laws, in a white man's world of legal justice, there is no question of leniency. Rudbeck has merely to let the hangman do his work and sign the death certificate; the role of executioner is not his legal responsibility. But Johnson pleads with Rudbeck as his friend and "father" to kill him, and Rudbeck does. He does it because he recognizes himself in Johnson: the poet, the dreamer, the builder of roads. He does it because he realizes he is as much the victim of law and order, rules and regulations, as Johnson is. He does it because he senses that by an accident of birth and color of skin he is the judge and Johnson the accused. He does it because as a colonialist he is Johnson's "father." Thus he allows Johnson the last vestige of dignity, a brave death which his body paralyzed by fear will not allow him:

Johnson knows then that he won't have to get up again from his knees. He feels the relief like a reprieve, unexpected, and he thanks Rudbeck for it. He triumphs in the greatness, the goodness, and the daring inventiveness of Rudbeck. All the force of his spirit is concentrated in gratitude and triumphant devotion; he is calling all the world to admit that there is no god like his god. He bursts out aloud "Oh Lawd, I tank you for my frien' Mister Rudbeck—de bigges' heart in de worl' " [page 225].

Early in the novel Johnson sings:

England is my country.
Oh, England, my home all on de big water.
Dat King of England is my King,
De bes' man in de worl', his heart is too big.
Oh, England, my home all on de big water [page 36].

At the end Johnson sings, " 'Goodbye, my sun. . . . my wind. . . . my rivers. . . . my father worl'. . . .

my mother sky. . . . my lil wife-night . . ." (pages
220-21). Rudbeck, as friend and "father and mother," as
judge and representative of the king, will execute him
personally because Johnson wants to die proudly for his
king, for his England, and not meanly for his crime of
murder.

Johnson's submissive death is the opposite of Louis
Aladai's defiant death. Johnson submits to the white man's
supremacy and blesses Rudbeck for his happiness while
Aladai rebels against the whites and curses them for his
unhappiness, but both hold on to the illusion that they
are destined for great things in a white man's world.
Johnson's surrender to death is the obverse of Aissa's
sacrifice; both surrender to a vision of glory to do something remarkable, "to perform some extraordinary feat of
sympathy and love, which . . . will have a definite effect
on the world" (page 225). Obai, in *An American Visitor*,
achieves his moment of glory by killing Bewsher; Johnson
achieves his "glorious destiny" by being killed.

Mister Johnson should be viewed as the final novel in
a series of novels on Africa which dramatize the various
facets of the African revolution. *Aissa Saved* explores the
conflicting religions and beliefs in the war of incompatible
ideals, particularly as they affect the mind and emotions
of Aissa, herself both product and victim of the revolution. *An American Visitor* examines the effect of conflicting cultures and ideas, particularly within the white
community, but everything the whites do and say also
deeply affects what the blacks do and say. In *The African
Witch* the battle is openly joined between the two races,
and this battle is dramatically focused on the conflict
within Aladai's mind between his white man's education
and his African origins. And finally, in *Mister Johnson*
Cary portrays the tragic effect of the revolution on the
susceptible and romantic mind of Johnson who, motivated
by the illusory vision of heroic destiny, in reality weaves
his own doom while believing he is a free man in a white
man's world.

Even though in his later novels Cary writes about England, the underlying theme is the same as in the African novels—the inexorable process of revolution which brings change for better and for worse in men's lives. In these later novels, as in the early novels, there is still a war on.

CHAPTER III

"THEY WANT TO BE HAPPY"

Castle Corner

*A*lthough *Castle Corner* (1938) was published the year before *Mister Johnson*, the last of the African novels, and although part of the action is set in Africa, it belongs to the next period of Cary's literary development. In its African scenes, it does seem to be a continuation of the "war" described in the early novels: the exploits of Harry "Cock" Jarvis in opening up new territory in Nigeria for trade parallel Cottee's direct actions in developing new mining territory as part of the African revolution described in *An American Visitor;* the primitive practices of ju-ju, human sacrifice, and tribal warfare are central to the meaning of *Aissa Saved* and *The African Witch*. A new element of the "war between cultures" is explored in *Castle Corner:* Cary develops the Conradian theme of the corrupting influence of the African environment on the white man; the weak-willed Major Kentish quickly degenerates and goes to seed in the tropical climate, but even the energetic and optimistic Hatto and the ambitious Felix Corner both eventually succumb and "go native." However, there is an essential difference between the African novels and the African element in *Castle Corner;* whereas the world of the African novels is largely an enclosed one, the African scenes in *Castle Corner* are reflections of the larger world of change and revolution outside Africa. The speculative stock market in African trading companies ruins amateurs like Felix and John Chass Corner and makes the fortune of a shrewd businessman like Benskin. The cockiness of Harry Jarvis in opening up Laka territory to trade causes an international incident and makes his reputation as a professional soldier; his professional soldier's attitude toward the Boer War turns his cousin Cleeve Corner to pacifism and radical politics and loses him his fiancée, Stella Pynsant. Cock Jarvis, as a conservative imperialist, has more in common with Jim Latter of *Not Honour More* than with Monkey Bewsher of *An American Visitor*. There is still a war on, but the war in Africa is seen in the perspective of larger historical events as they affect the lives of the characters in England and Ireland as well as Africa. The revolutionary changes that took place at the end of the nineteenth century are the background against which the lives of the characters are revealed.

The revolution in politics and art that is portrayed in *Castle Corner* emphasizes both the continuity of this novel with the African novels and the shift that has taken place in Cary's development as a novelist. In theme *Castle Corner* continues the exploration of the war of ideas, but the background of this conflict of beliefs is enlarged in scope to include the whole panorama of Anglo-Irish history—the Irish Land Acts, Home Rule, Parnell, imperialism, the Boer War, Radical politics, pacifism, and even the aesthetic movement, all of which have a direct impact on the lives of characters. In characterization the colonial types and the African characters are only a few of the many characters portrayed as each new generation seeks its own destiny in revolt against the old generation, creating the revolution that makes or destroys its happiness and the happiness of its elders. In form Cary attempts to achieve the complexity of the African novel series by using the family chronicle, contrasting individuals, families, and generations to explore the tremendous changes taking place in politics, economics, religion, art, science, and social customs.

Cary reveals in the preface to the Carfax edition that "*Castle Corner* was to have been the beginning of a vast work in three or four volumes showing not only the lives of all the characters in the first volume, but the revo-

lutions of history during the period 1880–1935." [1] He
further indicates that this scheme had already been
planned and much of it written, but he became dis-
couraged by the critical reception of *Castle Corner* and
abandoned the idea. The continuation of the series
is to be found among the manuscripts in the Osborn
Collection. The series was to have the general title "They
Want to Be Happy," and the individual volumes were
tentatively given the titles, *Castle Corner*, *Over the Top*,
and *Green Jerusalem*.[2] By examining in some detail this
scheme for a series of novels involving the characters of
Castle Corner, one can illustrate the significance of this
novel as a turning point in Cary's career and make clear
the reasons for its artistic failure.

Though *Castle Corner* contains some very fine scenes,
it is artistically the most diffuse and least satisfactory of
all his published novels. Part of the reason for its artistic
failure is, as Professor Wright points out, that "*Castle
Corner* has no central focus. Of the ninety-three characters who appear in the book, none dominates the story,
nor is there a sense that the generations of the Corner
family impinge upon one another enough to provide
continuity in this way." Castle Corner itself was intended
by Cary to provide that focus, both in the way if affects
the individual members of the Corner family and as a
symbol of revolutionary changes; it shifts from a large
wealthy estate to a decaying house and financial burden,
until at the end of the series it was to be turned into a
boarding house.[3] But Castle Corner is already crumbling
at the beginning of the novel and the old order which it
represents has already died before old John Chass Corner
dies and wills it to his well-meaning but incompetent son.
The characters, though affected by the castle and what it
signifies, are already committed to other ways of life
having different symbols and meanings.[4] Life at the castle
goes on, but its symbolic significance becomes diffuse as
the action moves to Africa or England, as the character
development shifts from the Corners to the Pynsants or

the Chorleys, as the battle of ideas changes from land economics to aesthetics or the Boer War and pacifism. The over-all plan of revealing the revolution, as it affects the lives of many characters in differing ways, defeats the symbolic purpose of Castle Corner. In *To Be a Pilgrim* Cary achieves the necessary balance between narration and symbol to create in Tolbrook Farm a meaningful symbol of the revolution and a structural focus for the novel. The question of who shall inherit Tolbrook becomes the question of who shall inherit England. The question of who shall inherit Castle Corner becomes the question of who shall inherit an anachronism.

Another reason why *Castle Corner* fails is that Cary intended its full meaning and impact to be closely dependent on the interrelationship of this novel with the others in the series. To some extent this is true of all multiple novels or novels in sequence: the interrelationship is an organic one in which each succeeding novel throws new light on the characters or the themes. But to be successful each novel of a series must stand alone. After the reader has completed all the novels of the series, he will perceive the larger pattern of the whole, but each novel must itself have organic unity. This is true of the African novels and of the novels in the two trilogies; it is not true of *Castle Corner*.

At the end of *Castle Corner* Cleeve Corner becomes involved in radical politics and pacifism in reaction to the Boer War, but there is no real indication that this commitment is any more permanent or deep than his involvement in the aesthetic movement. His conversion to the radical politics of Porfit (whom he despised until then) seems almost an accident of events rather than a conviction arising out of a personal crisis or deeply felt belief; rather than a committed partisan, he seems to be a young man of his time adopting the current fashions in ideas. Yet in the unpublished second volume of this series, *Over the Top*, we learn that Cleeve has made a successful career of politics. Cleeve is to develop in *Over the Top* from enthusiasm for freedom to disillusionment with people as a result of a libel action: he is *"forced into false position and this corrupts him. . . .* He becomes cynical in speech, is pushed to left." [5] He is financially ruined by the libel action and loses his wife Stella, who despises him when she learns the truth about his past, although she lies for him at the trial. [6]

The libel action which ruins Cleeve politically and financially is the scandal of his affair with Bridget Foy. In *Castle Corner* the affair is no more than one of Cleve's passing phases, a young man's lust and a young maid's trust in a promise to marry; to be sure Cleeve is remorseful, but his father and his uncle treat it more as a joke than a tragedy; and in a comic scene John Chass Corner, asserting the yet-existing powers of the landed gentry, bargains with the shrewd Rifty Egan to marry Bridget, and Cleeve is sent to Oxford. There is no indication that this episode is intended to haunt Cleeve later in life, ruin his political career, and break up his marriage.

Similarly, there is insufficient indication that Bridget is intended to be the prominent character she becomes in *Over the Top.* Cleeve becomes involved with her again because "he likes Finian [his illegitimate son by Bridget Foy] better than Stella's solid son and this estranges her." The attraction is Finian who later shocks Cleeve "by his bold mechanism, his denial of poetry, beauty, etc. his brutality as med. student." The new generation, though rooted in the old, revolts against its elders and continues the revolution, and ironically Cleeve has chosen to favor Finian over his legitimate children. Eventually Cleeve comes to realize the full nature of freedom—"freedom is evil as well as good." [7] In *Castle Corner* he had rebelled against the old order and had chosen a different way of life; in *Over the Top* he comes to represent the old order that is rebelled against by Finian representing the new generation, but now Cleeve has become conservative, seeing good in the old and evil in the new.

Cary does not go so far as to say that truth is an illusion, but he does explore the limitations of freedom and the illusion of permanent truths. Cleeve does not freely choose to go to Oxford and his indulgence of his passion for Bridget is intended to plague him years later in the second volume of the series. His attraction to Finian in *Over the Top* is partly a result of his sense of guilt, but he does not deliberately set out to destroy his own happiness with his wife. Stella wants to be happy, too, but she destroys her happiness with Cleeve because of jealousy and unforgiveness; no prisoner of grace, she fails him in the crisis, for though she perjures herself at the libel trial, the very act of perjury causes her to despise him.

There is a suggestion of fatalism in the melt game episode of *Castle Corner*. In a letter from Cary's father dated April 22, 1936, the melt game is explained: "I really forgot all about the maids game with herring milts of Castle Cary—they called them 'melts' and they used to talk, laugh over the shapes which they took when thrown against the whitewashed walls—I think it was just like 'telling their cups' when the tea leaves grouped themselves in various patterns." [8] Cary utilizes this game in the episode in which Sukey Egan foretells that Bridget will murder her, but nothing comes of the prophecy in the published novel, and it remains an interesting but minor and isolated anecdote of Irish folklore. In *Over the Top*, Matthew Egan (Rifty Egan of *Castle Corner*), Bridget's husband, dies of arsenic poisoning. Bridget is accused of murdering him and is arrested, but at the inquest she is acquitted for lack of evidence, although in the eyes of her neighbors she is guilty.[9]

Perhaps if Cary had carried out his original intention of taking the events of *Castle Corner* through 1910, many of these loose ends would have disappeared. But he stopped at 1900: already the manuscript was long, the material becoming unmanageable and intractable, and he expected that the projected succeeding volumes would clarify these points and develop others. There is no doubt that Cary chose the wrong method to develop his material, and having chosen the family chronicle he tried to make it do too much. An element of self-doubt is evident in his preface: "The criticism of *Castle Corner* . . . made me wonder if I had found the right means of saying what I had to say. I had learnt enough to know that the same general theme can be expressed in many different forms, but I had not fully realized that the very virtue of art, of which the power is that it can give experience, on that same account, limits its scope in argument" (page 5).

Though Cary insists he did not intend to write crude social philosophy but "meant to create characters and leave them to act," the idea if not the amount of the social and philosophical argument overshadows the development of characters as human beings and overwhelms the structure of the novel. The multiplicity of characters becomes a multiplicity of mutable ideas rather than a rich variety of life and experience; the controlling ideas of the castle symbol, the new search for happiness by each new generation, the war of beliefs, and changing fashions in ideas—all become diffuse in the multitude of incidents and plot developments.[10]

This diffusion is not lessened in the projected continuation. The lives of some of the older generation are rounded off, which in a family chronicle is more often through death than any other form of conclusion. Helen Pynsant, her degeneration indicated in *Castle Corner*, dies after a vulgar love affair; Benskin, her husband, achieves outward success and a measure of happiness in his son, but his love for Helen is destroyed. Hatto gains the wealth he sought in Africa, but loses his wife Daisy through death. Slatter gets rich and ends up a miser. Bridget inherits the castle because of Cleeve's son, but the castle is of no use to her; she dies and leaves all her money to the church. Sukey Egan dies. Cock Jarvis survives, only to lose Castle Corner and his hard-won power and glory.[11] But a host of new characters are in-

troduced as the new generation takes over—Mavis and
Dick, Cleeve's children; Edith, Hatto's daughter; Delia
Baskett and Eunice, friends of Cleeve and Stella.[12] His-
torical events are used directly to show the impact on the
lives of the characters and to illustrate the war of ideas.
In *Over the Top* the Irish Civil War deeply affects the
Anglo-Irish characters; the Russian Revolution is greeted
at first with enthusiasm by Cleeve and later with dis-
enchantment; the cause of women's rights is taken up by
Cock Jarvis; and in the third volume, *Green Jerusalem*,
Cleeve becomes an enthusiastic supporter of British
socialism until the violence of the general strike in the
1930's disillusions him again.[13]

It is doubtful whether Cary could ever have successfully controlled all this material: it is too vast and
diffuse, too broad and unfocused in character and incident. The extant unpublished manuscripts reveal no
solution. The material itself overwhelmed and defeated
him as a novelist. He does attempt to overcome one of the
weaknesses of *Castle Corner* by making Cleeve Corner
and Cock Jarvis more dominant characters in *Over the
Top* and *Green Jerusalem*, but the pattern of diversified
settings, characters, and events established in *Castle
Corner* foils this attempt to control the material. By the
time he came to write *To Be a Pilgrim*, only four years
later, Cary had discovered the method by which to
control the material of the past in conflict with the revolutionary present.

Part of Cary's difficulty with the *Castle Corner* series
was that he not only tried to develop the numerous
threads of his story in *Castle Corner* and at the same time
project them into the later volumes, but he also incorpo-
rated material from an earlier uncompleted work entitled
Cock Jarvis, a vast, rambling novel of nearly a half million
words. Cock Jarvis and some of the other characters were
used in *Castle Corner*—e.g., Cleeve Corner, Stella,
Bridget Foy, John Chass Corner, Giveen, and Jingler.
Some of the Irish scenes in *Castle Corner* were suggested

by material in *Cock Jarvis*, and there are notes on Irish
land laws, Parnell, and the Parnellites, a description of a
pheasant shoot, a newspaper clipping giving information
on inquests, and even lists of current slang for 1892 and
1910, all originally intended for *Cock Jarvis* but used in
Castle Corner.[14] The bulk of material from *Cock Jarvis*
appears in the African scenes in *Over the Top* and *Green
Jerusalem* as well as in *Castle Corner*. Harry Jarvis' ex-
ploit of going into Daji against orders is found in *Cock
Jarvis;* his later career as a political agitator and supporter
of woman's suffrage is utilized in the projected volumes.
The cockiness of Jarvis the soldier in *Castle Corner*
becomes the cockiness of Jarvis the war hero, imperialist,
and political agitator in *Over the Top* and *Green
Jerusalem.* As in *Cock Jarvis* Porfit and Cleeve Corner
become interested in the colonies for political reasons,
and thus the opposition between Cleeve and his cousin
Jarvis is established on a political as well as a personal
level in *Over the Top* and *Green Jerusalem.*

   Though *Castle Corner* is an artistic failure, it is of
great significance to the development of Cary as a novelist. A novel of transition, it separates his African novels
from his later books and represents a crisis of failure
after which he matured as a novelist. In the preface to
The African Witch Cary says, "after I finished the
American Visitor I decided to write no more books about
Africa. I was actually planning Castle Corner, to cover a
wider scene . . . when my agents asked me for another
African book, and I reflected that it would be easy to
complete the Black Prince before I finished the great
amount of preparation needed for the *Castle Corner*
monument." [15] After completing *The African Witch*,
Cary returned to the *Castle Corner* series, but when the
critical reception of *Castle Corner* raised doubts in his
mind about the validity of the projected series, he
"abandoned the whole enterprise, and turned to write
about the simplest of characters in a simple background,
with the simplest of themes, Mister Johnson, the artist of

his own joyful tale" (page 8). Though he confesses to a regret at "the loss of my characters in *Castle Corner*," Cary as a writer was released from the burden of that unmanageable material. With *Mister Johnson* Cary achieves a lyrical style that is developed in *A House of Children* and a simplicity of structure and characterization that is used successfully in *Charley Is My Darling*.

Mister Johnson is the last of the African novels, but already with *Castle Corner* Cary had broken away from the limitations of the African setting. Furthermore, in the early 1930's Cary attempted to deal with non-African material in the unpublished but completed *Arabella*, a poorly written political satire that ends as a naïve fantasy about a bolshevized America, and in the fragmentary but better written *Marta*.[16] Both of these unpublished works indicate Cary's early desire to broaden the scope of his writings and try something wholly unrelated to his African experience.

Without his attempt to write the *Castle Corner* series Cary would have been less prepared to write the two trilogies, but by abandoning the series Cary freed himself to experiment with different styles (the present tense of *Mister Johnson* and *Charley Is My Darling*), with different points of view (the autobiographical first person of *A House of Children* and the objectification of the first-person narration in the first trilogy), and with a different approach to the multiple novel. *Castle Corner* anticipates the future direction of Cary's writing career in the two novels of childhood and the first trilogy while at the same time it takes one more look at the African scene from the perspective of history. It is a novel of transition, not merely from the African setting to the Anglo-Irish setting, but from the "old fashioned or dramatic" plots, which he felt his African material required, to the more experimental novels of the later period.

CHAPTER IV

"THE CHILD IS A BORN CREATOR"

Charley Is My Darling
A House of Children

*A*lthough Cary's next two published novels, *Charley Is My Darling* (1940) and *A House of Children* (1941), represent a complete break from the African setting, they show a continuity of development with the two preceding novels, *Castle Corner* and *Mister Johnson*. Charley Brown is the soulmate of Mister Johnson. Both are described in the present tense because both live for the moment, enjoying the freedom they create for themselves, yet trapped by the consequences of actions which made them free; the very style links them together as free individual spirits, poets of the moment, improvising imaginatively the actions which become the pattern of their unhappy destinies. Both want to be liked and admired by their contemporaries and their superiors, but in trying to gain the approval of others they destroy their own happiness; both find expression for their imaginations in criminal actions and are inevitably caught by the reckless daring which excites their creative minds; both are romantics who are destroyed by the conflict of their romanticism with reality.

Similarly, *A House of Children* is related to *Castle Corner*. Aside from the obvious duplication of the setting in northern Ireland at the same time (1890) and the use of the same family, the Corners (though a different branch), *A House of Children* is closely related to *Castle Corner* in the development of certain aspects of theme and character. It is not that Cary, having abandoned the *Castle*

Corner series, decided to salvage and use what he could from the unpublished material he had written as a continuation; there is no such relationship between that material and *A House of Children*, as there exists between the unpublished *Cock Jarvis* manuscript and *Castle Corner*. Rather, it is that Cary, having written *Castle Corner* and worked on its continuation, came to see the possibilities of shaping the raw material of his own youth into fiction. Castle Corner is Castle Cary, the ancestral home of Cary's family, and the Corners are the Carys, the Anglo-Irish landlords ruined by the Irish land acts of the 1880's.[1]

In *Castle Corner* the autobiographical material is objectified by the emphasis on the revolutionary changes taking place in the lives of the fictional characters and the war of ideas which these lives illustrate. The use of the third person reinforces the historical objectivity of the action and the detachment of the narrative. *A House of Children*, on the other hand, is more frankly autobiographical. Cary, in the preface to the Carfax edition, says, "I am asked often if the book is autobiography. The answer is that names, places, and people are disguised, because many of the people are living."[2] The implication is that except for the disguised names, the novel is autobiographical, but as with all autobiographical fiction it would be misleading (as well as unrewarding) to read it as autobiography. Art, Cary says in *Art and Reality*, is a partial view of reality; the obverse of this is that life is never so shaped and formed as art. Something of this is revealed in Cary's next statement in the preface: "I have given myself an elder brother. . . . I notice that this elder brother is also myself, and I suspect that I divided myself in this way because I realized by some instinct (it was certainly not by reason) that the two together as a single character would be too complex for the kind of book I needed to write" (page 7).

The approach to reality which the novelist wishes to make—whether subjective and experiential as in *A House*

of Children or objective and ideational as in *Castle Corner*—determines the narrative technique he will use. Two
discarded beginnings for *Castle Corner*, both written in
the first person, show the underlying similarity of the
material and the results achieved by different techniques:

People still pity the Victorian child. They say, the Victorian
age may have been a great age but it was a bad one for
children. But I think perhaps a great age is always good for
children because a great age is one that knows its own mind
and can answer questions. When I was young I believed that
the wicked went to hell and the good to Heaven. This didn't
trouble me in the least but it settled questions that might have
troubled me, and spoilt my happiness.

Of course I didn't know that I was living in a great age,
or any kind of age. People do not live in an age; it is part of
them and they are part of it. I remember only people, houses,
things; nice people, unfriendly people; delightful or boring
houses; and interesting things. The other things I have forgotten.

The kindest person lived in the most delightful house. This
was aunt Mary Corner who lived at Castle Corner in Annish,
which is in the North of Ireland.[3]

A more direct and less introspective version begins as
follows:

Castle Corner is in Annish, which is the most northern part
of Ireland. It used to be a good place for children. It had
many attics, and deep cellars, fields and woods. . . . It stood
on the shore and there were three boats. Mr. and Mrs. John
Charles Corner were both spoilers of children; tho' in different ways, for Mr. Corner let them do what they liked, and
Mrs. Corner took trouble to make them happy. We relied
upon her when we were in trouble; sick; and when we didn't
know what to do with ourselves. At other times, of course,
we paid no attention to her at all. We were full of our own
affairs which occupied every moment of our time.[4]

The resemblance of both passages—the introspective and
interpretative commentary of the first and the sense of
an enclosed child's world in the second—to the beginning

of *A House of Children* is readily apparent, whereas both passages are quite different in point of view, tone, and style from the published version of *Castle Corner*.

The third-person narration of *Charley Is My Darling* illustrates further the transformation that occurs when a different technique is used to approach similar material. Although the 1890 world of the Corner children in *A House of Children* seems far removed from Charley's experiences as a wartime slum child who has been evacuated from London, both novels deal with essentially the same basic theme: "the child is a born creator"[5] living in a world apart, isolated from the adult world by his imagination yet betrayed by that adult world because he seeks to create his own world. However, in *Charley Is My Darling* the third-person point of view objectifies this isolation and betrayal, while in *A House of Children* the first-person viewpoint makes it subjective and introspective.

Charley Brown at the very beginning of the novel is immediately set apart from the other children by the fact that he is louse-ridden and his hair must be completely shaved off. Anthony West, reviewing the novel in the *New Yorker*, severely criticizes Cary for basing his narrative on the adverse reactions of the other children to Charley's lice and his shaved head, for Mr. West assures us that being louse-ridden was a common experience to the evacuees who, therefore, would be indifferent to such a natural phenomenon.[6] Mr. West may be correct about the incidence of lice among London slum children evacuated to the country during the war, but he misses the point Cary uses as the catalyst for his narrative—the cruelty of the child's imagination which seizes upon the vulnerability of the stranger and outsider, his differentness of the moment, whether it be his clothes, his speech, or the glasses he wears (taunting him with the chant "four-eyes," as Charley is taunted, and hurting him no matter how many other children wear glasses, statistically speaking).[7] As Cary states it in more general terms in a note found among the manuscripts: "Tragedy of children. From outside and inside. May be cruelty and hatred. May . . . be ignorance, inability. . . . May be cruelty of one child to another. May be inevitable differences of power, beauty, felt more bitterly by children, who have not devised escapes." [8] Charley Brown will not be accepted into the gang until he proves himself either through physical strength or the power of his wits.

Cary notes:

Charley is used to a social life in the streets. His idea of happiness is social; to have friends, to give friendship. He wants to be liked & admired and he is ready, on his side, to admire almost any kind of skill or distinction. He suffers when he finds himself alone, and like other . . . people, he struggles to create for himself a society, both of dreams and reality, in which he shall have his place. [9]

Thus Charley, because he is creative, uses his fertile imagination to overcome the initial hostility of the gang and gain acceptance into the group; through his superior imagination he is even accepted as leader, however tentatively, and because of this he must continue to prove himself by his exploits.

Like Mister Johnson, Charley Brown involves himself more and more deeply in criminal actions because they are a daring outlet for his energy, courage, and imagination. Cary notes, "He is interested in the creative idea and could use it in art if the idea of art were opened to him. But it is not opened." [10] He becomes, like Johnson, the artist of his own destiny. Neither of them is a hardened criminal although they are both judged as such by society; they are both led astray by their desire for acceptance in a world that does not accept them and so each creates "a society, both of dreams and reality, in which he shall have his place." [11]

The other boys are contrasts to Charley, foils to his creative imagination. Harry, while he shares Charley's enthusiasm, lacks his confidence and imagination; Ginger, though he is more practical than either Charley or Harry, is more indifferent, untroubled by Harry's doubts but more easily led; Bill and Mort gain leadership by physical domination and cruelty, but both give way, however reluctantly, to Charley's superior imagination. Bill is crude and cruel in contrast to Charley's sensitivity, yet it is he who reforms while Charley becomes more and more deeply involved in criminal actions, and though Mort is more deliberately cruel and violent than all the others, he is defeated by Charley in a fight. They are cruel and violent children, yet they are capable of loyalty and love. Their delinquency and distorted values are found in the adult world, particularly in Galor's righteous beating of his daughter Liz, in the degeneracy of Charley's mother, and in Lina Allchin's confused and misguided handling of Charley.

Charley needs love and understanding which Lina cannot give him because she is governed by her modern ideas rather than by her instincts. In his own romantic world Charley finds the love and understanding which is denied to him by the adult world. Liz Galor, like the idea of art, represents Charley's search for love and goodness in life; he offers her the loot from the burglaries as an expression of his love. The love of Charley and Liz is a mixture of childhood affection and loyalty and adult passion. It is the natural expression of their fondness for each other during the awkward years between childhood and adulthood, but the outcome, Liz's pregnancy, is viewed with horror by the adults, even by Lina Allchin. At the end both Charley and Liz have matured and are ready to accept responsibility for themselves, but adult society brands them as delinquent children. Charley, aware of his coming adulthood, asks "wy don they leave us alone"? Liz, aware of her lost childhood, answers, "cos we're kids." She does not want them to change but knows they will because life itself will change them.

In *Charley Is My Darling* Cary concentrates on a single character and a single theme. The simplicity of construction in both novels, after the complexity of *Castle Corner*, was an exploration of technique by which Cary sought to achieve greater control over his material before again attempting the complexity of the trilogy form. In *A House of Children* Cary experimented with one more technique—the first person.

The first-person narrator who looks back on his childhood and youth and interprets as he reexperiences is traditional in the English novel; it is particularly suited to the developmental novel with its emphasis on the growing awareness of the narrator. The rationale of the first-person point of view in the autobiographical novel is succinctly stated by Cary in a passage included in the manuscript versions of *A House of Children:*

A childs recollections are like separate dabs of paint on a canvas; he sees each dab vividly; but he does not see any necessary connections between it and others. It is only long afterwards, when his faith and memory gives him the shape and lengthness of the original column . . . that he sees this connection; sees the future. So I perceived all at once not only how much I owed to this forgotten tutor [Pinto Freeman] but that all the events of my time with him make an episode.[12]

The children of this novel are not the delinquents of *Charley Is My Darling*; they live in an ordered world where right and wrong behavior is clearly defined. They are born creators like Charley Brown, and although they show some of his reckless daring, they have open to them the world of art through their plays and poems, a means of self-expression and self-discovery that is denied to Charley. Like the evacuees, they are "all trying to *learn* and longing to *know*—but at the same time continually deceived by grown ups," but the deception leads to self-knowledge, not self-destruction as it does for Charley. The Corner children have their aunts, who represent stability and order, affection and love no matter how much they may disappoint, and they have their tutor Pinto, whose "sense of life, of beauty, of drama, & his immense curiosity & respect for learning"[13] provide an

outlet for their creative energies, although he may dis-
illusion them as a hero. Charley Brown has only Lina Allchin who, when she deceives him, destroys his chance to
learn creatively.

Evelyn Corner, the narrator, looking back on the meaning of his childhood experiences with the perspective of
a mature man, reexperiences the sensations of childhood
and reinterprets them to discover the pattern of his life.
A branch of fuschia "waving stiffly up and down in the
breeze" is the Proustlike correspondence that releases the
remembrance of things past: "at once I smelt the breeze
salty, and had a picture of a bright curtain flapping in-
wards and, beyond the curtain, dazzling sunlight on miles
of crinkling water. I felt too, expectancy so keen that it
was like a physical tightening of the nerves; the very
sense of childhood" (page 9). But to the narrator it is
only a moment grasped out of the flux of sensations that
is childhood, "a piece of life, unique and eternal" that
must be interpreted by the mature man, for children "do
not even live consciously, they exist; they drift through
sensations as a pantomime fairy passes through coloured
veils and changing lights" (page 9).

Unlike *Charley Is My Darling*, *A House of Children* is
narrated in the past tense in order to achieve the perspective of historical time. The narrator comments on the
meaning of his life as a child: the joyful expectancy of
new experiences and new ideas ("we were growing
drunk with expectation. . . . All day one would live in
the sense of something to come") is "the natural state of
children, to whom everything comes as discovery, and to
whom discovery is a keen pleasure" (page 28). These
comments are not obtrusive because they are an integral
part of the narrating consciousness, because they reveal
the pattern of discovery underneath the episodic flux of
experience, because they grow out of the content of the
children's lives—and because they are kept to a minimum.
In revision Cary curbed a tendency to expound and philo-
sophize. The following passage is in the published text:

We had our Bible lessons, of course, but the religion which actually stayed with us was something livelier, braver, keener than the Church teaching; and much more real. A lecture from a boy's parent, a sailor, about chasing slave dhows in the Gulf, went to the bottom of our feelings at one flash" [page 34].

The passage below, which continues from the above passage, was discarded:

Sermons about temperance or charity left behind them only a sense of boredom. Something within us knew at once what was dead and negative; what was positive and living and the same silent critic knew too, without always making it plain to our minds, the difference between the time serving non-sense often preached to us and purposive talk of the sailor. We did not say that the Church religion was already rotten with evasion, with moral cowardice, with dodging the real issues of a real world. We had no idea of the real world or its issues. We were highly respectful to all clergy. But we felt also that our masters when they talked of freedom and justice or the sailor when he described the quality of the slave trade, and demanded more ships to stop it, knew what they meant. They had a faith, which was alive even in their voices.[14]

The discarded passage is too abstract, and while the narrator insists that the children knew all this instinctively rather than intellectually, it is a dubious device to get around the inarticulateness of children. The narrator's commentary is obtrusive, and Cary wisely deleted it from the final version.

Similarly, the important passage at the end of Chapter 64, in which the narrator interprets the poetic experience of a church service and the religious experience of Shakespeare's poetry, was condensed from an elaborate philosophical passage:

So bits of the church service remained with me because they were poetry. They gave me the feeling of beauty and wisdom joined together in one unity of experience. But no prayer or poem had so powerful an effect as my first great Shakespeare play. *I'm told that primitive religion is full of*

*dramatic ritual & that plays themselves began as religious
rites. I can well understand that, for if religion aims at telling
real truth by direct experience, which is the only way to
convey a truth about reality, facts of course are a different
matter since they are not real themselves: they are only about
something real, (i.e. "that chair" is descriptive of a phenom-
enal form or shape whose real nature is unknown) thus it
has no other means than poetry, music, light, colour, form
and dramatic ritual; for nothing else gives a direct experience
of "goodness," "badness," "love," "beauty" and other real
elements of living.*

*So I suppose that the intensity of my excitement during the
play was simply a strong religious experience.* When I heard
the cry: "All lost, to prayers, to prayers," and the line: "What,
must our mouths be cold," I *felt* death as if I had never heard
of it before. *I don't mean by a religious experience, a moral
experience. I doubt if any child can have a moral experience.
. . . It happened to me only as an experience, rich and
strong, of the real life of the world; of death . . . love,
beauty, ugliness, cruelty, so that I was moved by a conflict of feelings that I came up from the first scene like one
who had been ducked in deep water, blown out with be-
wildering truth.*[15]

As in *Aissa Saved*, Cary saw the necessity for cutting
down the philosophizing.

Revision is essential to the writer; it often makes the
difference between artistic achievement or failure, an
exercise of literary and artistic judgment of which the
reader is unaware, for he sees only the end result on the
printed page and not the critical faculty at work in revision. Cary constantly revised his manuscripts, dis-
carding whole chapters and scenes, writing new ones and
revising them, changing words and sentences to tighten
the writing stylistically, developing characters who in
revision become more significant or even dropping some
who in revision become unimportant. A projection into
the future of one of the children is discarded as unnecessary—Kathy "afterwards a suffragette, a modern girl." [16]
A character's dominant trait—"Cousin Philip is the devil
who drips cynicism and spoils things for us"—is tem-

pered by present understanding of motives and feelings.
A scene is transformed—the delightfully comic fiasco of
the children's play is developed from a more sketchy
original version. An important sentence is changed to
delete the extraneous abstract explanation—"Harry had
made a sudden leap ahead of me *which was like jumping
out of childhood into youth; out of a life of a dream-like
sensuous experience, into a critical analysis and ar-
guing.*" [17] A long passage is discarded and completely re-
written (the whole of Chapter 18). A sentence is added
in revision to explain further the remembered sensation of
crawling through a tunnel—"I don't remember whether
our pit in the garden showed clay or gravel, but I remember the sensation of wriggling through the tunnel, of
dead weight hanging above me" (page 38).

The exploration of Shell Port cave represents the child's
exploration of the world—the physical closeness, the
stimulation to the imagination, the groping toward knowledge, the chance remark that consolidates the sensations
into an idea. Anketel, the youngest of the children, when
asked why he tries to lift the water up with his feet,
answers, "I was only feeling at it," and the narrator comments, "I was thirty years older before I appreciated the
force of the 'at'" (page 54). The pattern is there, but it
is only perceived much later by the adult mind, because
the passage from childhood to maturity is not an ordered pattern progressing from year to year. In the discarded version of Chapter 18, Cary wrote, "Childhood
ends only with responsibility, & the serious effort to
grasp the world in general ideas goes with responsibility.
The passage from the life of live sensation into that of
ideal conception is discontinuous; it goes by jerks." [18]
Thus, Evelyn Corner's childhood does not suddenly end
at eight when he and the red-cheeked boy decide that the
Maylin party is childish and they are too old for silly
games. "I didn't stop being a hopeful and foolish child,"
the narrator comments, but like Leila in Katherine Mansfield's story, "My First Ball," Evelyn Corner is "drawn

aside for a moment from the stream of childish sensation and made to feel his separation from it" (page 67).

Cary gives Evelyn an older brother, Harry, to objectify and reinforce the pattern of change that must inevitably come. The passage from childhood to maturity becomes the pattern of the novel. It happens to Robert when he goes off to school, as it had happened earlier to Cousin Philip: "Robert was out of our lives, and Harry was our senior" (page 57). Frances, who seems at times childishly flighty, is next; she marries MacKee of whom she and the younger children made fun, and devotes herself to being a wife and mother. Then Delia, to whom the younger children look for leadership, deserts them and runs off to marry Pinto. And at the end Harry makes his sudden leap ahead of Evelyn, as Evelyn will ahead of Anketel. This over-all pattern of successive passages from childhood to maturity is the connection between the "separate dabs of paint" on the canvas of life; the separate dabs, the isolated crises and individual changes are what give texture, variety, and complexity to the portrait of childhood that Cary paints in this novel.

Cary's view of childhood is not sentimental, but neither is it cynical. To him childhood is a time of experiment in living before the pattern is set, of eagerness for experiences before the excitement and the novelty wear off, of creative imagination before it is lost in the perplexity of adulthood when the grown man comes to realize that "there is no time to begin again, to get things right" (page 67).

In the original version of Chapter 18 it is the children's faces that are sad because "sadness is the ground of their living"; the greater the children's power of enjoyment, the greater "their feeling of the waste of life, of happiness, of youth & love, of themselves." [19] In the published version it is the grown-ups' faces that are sad because there is no time for a new beginning. Thus in revising the chapter Cary emphasizes the theme that it is the adult who feels the waste of life and the child who sees life as endless. The original version is closer to the sense of the loneliness and isolation of childhood revealed in *Charley Is My Darling*, but the published version is more consistent with the sense of the novelty and the anticipation of experience portrayed in *A House of Children*. The published text underscores the main theme of the novel: the child is a born creator; the adult is the made critic of life.

Cary's most creative personalities are children, whatever their chronological ages: Mister Johnson; Charley Brown; Evelyn Corner and his alter ego, his brother Harry; Sara Monday; and Gulley Jimson. In *Mister Johnson* and *Charley Is My Darling* the reader himself is the critic although his judgment is suspended by the use of the present tense. In *A House of Children* the critical judgment is achieved by the split function of the narrator recreating the actual sensations of his childhood and revealing the pattern from the perspective of adulthood. In his next work Cary uses the first-person narrative to portray the immediate experience and the subjective point of view and the form of the trilogy to achieve perspective and objectivity.

CHAPTER V

"FREEDOM AS CREATION"
THE FIRST TRILOGY

Herself Surprised
To Be a Pilgrim
The Horse's Mouth

Herself Surprised, Cary writes in his prefatory essay to the Carfax edition, "is the first book of a trilogy which was designed to show three characters, not only in themselves but as seen by each other. The object was to get a three-dimensional depth and force of character. One character was to speak in each book and describe the other two as seen by that person. . . . The centre of the plan was character." [1] Each novel of the trilogy is a full portrait of a character, narrated in the first person from the point of view of the protagonist; each portrait is different because of Cary's ability to enter into the character portrayed. This negative capability, one of Cary's most important talents as a novelist, was his ability to *be* Sara Monday (*Herself Surprised*), an earthy woman who lives by a code of natural morals but who also has a natural capacity for love and forgiveness; to be Tom Wilcher (*To Be a Pilgrim*), the man whom history and change left behind but whose basic wisdom and moral experience enable him to survive and be a pilgrim in a modern world that is drifting aimlessly; and to be Gulley Jimson (*The Horse's Mouth*), a reprobate artist who speaks from the horse's mouth about art and the artist in conflict with society. Though it does not depend upon these approaches, Cary's ability to submerge

67

his own ego into the personality he creates is best illustrated in the trilogy form and the first person point of
view. The form of the trilogy enabled Cary to develop
the narrating personalities fully, each according to his or
her point of view, yet at the same time he could achieve
complexity because the themes and the characters of each
novel of the trilogy are further developed in the other
two novels.

Cary says of art and reality that "every character in
every situation is significant to some degree, because all
of them are part of the one real world in action." But, he
goes on to say, "it is impossible to show this whole in one
book. James Joyce has tried in *Finnegans Wake* to give
this notion of reality in depth; for that purpose, he devised a special language, and still he had to leave out nine-
tenths of what is significant even by his own scheme."
Therefore, "the great problem before a writer is to convey, in one work of art, one formal conception, a significance which is simple enough for immediate apprehension by the feelings of a reader, and yet not false to the
immense complication of actual life." [2] Both Conrad and
James sought to render "the immense complication of
actual life" by ordering that reality through the analytical
mind and emotional sensibility of a single narrator. In his
trilogies Cary conveys the complexity of reality by presenting three alternative views of that reality.

In practice the trilogy form has its limitations. According to his original plan the first trilogy "was to consist of
two personal confessions by people of narrow education
but strong feeling; and, in the centre . . . a much larger
work giving the general political and religious scene of
the period, & especially the character of the English civilization." [3] Thus *To Be a Pilgrim*, chronologically and
thematically in the middle, in Cary's analogy, was to
serve the same function as the large central panel of a
triptych. *Herself Surprised* and *The Horse's Mouth*
were to correspond to the narrow side panels. In another

unpublished note Cary explains this in more detail:

> As Sara, the individualist, in the first section of the book, the narrow side panel, so to speak, on the left of the main picture, stands outside society, but knows how to make use of it for her own ends; so Gulley, the individualist in the third corresponding section, on the right, stands outside society, but, for the good of his soul, despises it, fears it and is always in danger of hating it. He is obliged to admonish himself continually "Forgive it, for it is a blind fool." He is the extreme of the English spirit in his anarchism, his profound loneliness of soul, his sense of the immediate real; a protestant to the bone. He is the artist Gulley in his inability to make terms with society.[4]

In actuality, the trilogy is similar and at the same time different from the triptych; the analogy is useful in illuminating Cary's intentions, but it would be less than useful if it were taken as the ultimate revelation of form rather than as a metaphor of intention. *To Be a Pilgrim* is the longest novel of the three, but it is not much longer than *The Horse's Mouth*. It is the central panel "giving the general political and religious scene of the period," but it does not dominate the whole so that the reader is drawn to it as the central focus to which the "side panels" contribute their supporting stories. Perhaps in part *To Be a Pilgrim* only seems to be the lesser achievement because its narrator, Tom Wilcher, is the more passive personality by reason of his introspective role whereas Gulley Jimson is the more forceful personality by reason of his "strong feeling." But nonetheless it seems clear that *The Horse's Mouth*, because of its more complex theme, its structure which recapitulates the whole trilogy. and its rich language which gives meaning to the whole, is the greater creative triumph. The intended analogy to the triptych form is weakened by the superb artistic achievement of *The Horse's Mouth* as one of the "side" panels, which draws attention from *To Be a Pilgrim* as the central panel, but no reader would want *The Horse's*

Mouth to be less than the achievement it is in order to
save the truism of an analogy.

In a note Cary says:

> The trilogy was planned before Herself Surprised was
> written, but it was not published as planned. Sara, Wilcher and
> Gulley were all partly realized characters in different sketches
> and the trilogy was a separate enterprise intended to shew
> the same world over the same period of time from three
> different points of view. It was an idea formed, that is,
> before characters came into it. . . . The object was to do
> something which has, I think not been achieved in a novel, to
> give history a three dimensional depth, not as a comparison
> of accidents, but a related order of change.[5]

As Cary states in the preface to *Herself Surprised*, the
scheme "did not come off." It failed because "when I let
Sara talk about art and history I found that she lost something of her quality and force; the essential Sara was
diluted" (page 7). But this imbalance of the three characters in the first trilogy—at least when compared to the
original plan—does not mean that the trilogy form fails.
The three novels are interrelated in theme, character,
technique, and style; and each novel, though separate in
its own right, adds its necessary part to the composition
of the whole. The trilogy form has its limitations—the
ideal scheme "made the books too long, & at a certain
point of development, actually decreased the force &
drive of realisations" [6]—but the first trilogy is a successful artistic achievement.

HERSELF SURPRISED (1941)

Sara Monday is herself surprised, surprised by life with
its variety, patterns, ironies, successes, and failures. Who
would have thought that this girl who had come from a
good home, her father a freeholder and working fore-
man and her mother a teacher, and who had won prizes

for recitation and Scripture and been granted a certificate for sewing would be castigated by a judge as an "unhappy example of that laxity and contempt for all religious principle and social obligation which threatens to undermine the whole fabric of our civilization" (page 9). Yet by the end of *Herself Surprised* Sara is revealed as a woman with a high moral sense. As Cary says of Sara in an essay, "her morals were the elementary morals of a primitive woman, of nature herself, which do not change." Her life, Cary continues, is "constructive, creative. She builds a society, a relationship, a spiritual world"[7] for herself and her man. It is a creative life, and therefore a free one. But, paradoxically, she is a prisoner of society.

Each of the three narrators in the trilogy is a prisoner. Gulley Jimson (just out of prison) is a prisoner of his art. Tom Wilcher (who is threatened with "imprisonment" in an asylum) is a prisoner of the past. Sara Monday (who is being sentenced to a prison term) is a prisoner of grace. In *Herself Surprised* we learn from Sara that she stole the goods in order to help Gulley and his son. In *To Be a Pilgrim* we learn from Tom Wilcher that the things she stole are mere "trinkets" and "useless trifles" and that he blames himself for not paying her enough wages; Sara had come to him when he was a lost soul and saved him from despair. And in *The Horse's Mouth* we learn from Gulley Jimson that Sara has forgiven him the physical cruelty which leads to her death; she gives the police a deliberately wrong description, thus protecting Gulley from a manslaughter charge.

Each novel contributes its partial view of Sara, each true in its own context; together they make a composite portrait of Sara Monday, the element of grace and forgiveness in this world. We see Sara as she sees herself, "the victim of mysterious events and her own soft heart; as Wilcher sees her (in *To Be a Pilgrim*), the devoted and unselfish servant and mistress; as Jimson sees her (in *The Horse's Mouth*), cunning, vain, lecherous, self-

deceiving, a man-catcher . . ." (page 8). Similarly, we
see Gulley Jimson with Sara's eyes and readjust our views
of their relationship and our understanding of Gulley as
a man (but not as an artist) as revealed in *The Horse's
Mouth*. We see Tom Wilcher with Sara's eyes and readjust our views of him as a lecherous old man with a pen-
chant for servants (but not as the historian of the heritage
of the past) as suggested in *To Be a Pilgrim*.

In a series of notes among the manuscript versions of
the trilogy, Cary further amplifies Sara's character.
"Sara is unselfish and looks forward—is detached from
ambition and never stops to think of herself." Sara, like
Gulley, is "an enjoyer of the moment, with pangs."
She has a sense of fatalism, for she "feels I'm myself and
I can't help it. . . .With Gulley, perhaps it was appointed
and who am I to make a fuss when he beats her . . . it
was owed to me." [8] It is an animistic view of morality:

[Sara] acts in a hurry, on the impulse to make a . . . bit of
happiness for her man, & to save a peaceful world. She studies
the man for this reason, gives way to him—but is obstinate in
saving her own world. . . . Sara deceives Matt to make a
kind of happiness, to bring him out, so also with Gylee
[Gulley] and Willsher [Wilcher]—to make a world *Not*
devoted to him alone—but to an ideal of which he is part.
Seeks what is fitting for him & all unconsciously.[9]

When she first meets Gulley (who moves into the
house with luggage, paints, and wife), Sara is disap-
pointed. Gulley is not her romantic idea of an artist although she has not seen an artist before. He is "a little
bald man with a flat nose and a big chin. His head was big
and hung over so that his face was hollow in the middle.
He was much older than we expected, getting on for
forty; very shabby too, and had a front tooth missing"
(page 41). What attracts her is his simple and gay love of
life and his free, independent spirit; he was "not one to
care what the world thinks." She knows nothing of art
except insofar as she reflects current public taste; she

thinks his paintings are ugly, even the famous portrait for which she had reluctantly posed.[10]

The artist Gulley does not need a personal relationship with Sara to create, but he does need beauty, and this Sara provides him. She complements and inspires him (for a while at least, until he has gone on to something else, and then he feels the relationship she has built around him is a prison to his creative freedom). She is not herself beautiful (if truth be told, she is a bit dumpy-looking), but Gulley's portrait of her shows beauty. Conventionally prim, Sara is amazed that Nina, Gulley's wife, could calmly sit in the same room while she poses partly in the nude and that Gulley could look at her coldly "as if I had been a statue." She surprises herself:

> It seemed to me then that I had been a fool to be so prim before and yet I wondered at myself. I could not tell whether I had done a religious thing or a bad one. When I went home again, I was in wonder and dismay all the evening. I thought: "What will I do next?—there seems to be nothing I wouldn't do" [page 59].

She had done a religious thing, for she had inspired an artist; she had done a bad thing, for her husband Matt Monday accuses her of being Gulley's mistress.

Sara is basically a religious person, but her deepest religious feelings are creative rather than conventional. Her "feeling that people should *get their right*," Cary writes in an unpublished note, "is a feeling for freedom—i.e. their development. She combines this with a certain lawlessness because [she is] in natural conflict with law." [11] Thus, years later, after she has left Gulley, she steals from Tom Wilcher, not out of economic necessity or avarice but in order to help Gulley get his paints and canvases and to support his son Tommy, for she understood intuitively that in a real sense society owed Gulley a living as an artist. She does not articulate this view, but her deep sense of justice and her woman's heart move her to feel pity and compassion for Gulley, who has no one else to take care of him. Besides, she reasons, Tom Wilcher would not miss the few old things she took and if he did he would not really mind.

Sara's capacity for love and life is her salvation as well as her undoing; her capacity for forgiveness and compassion is our saving grace as well as our shame. By the end of *Herself Surprised* we know Sara to be a woman with a high moral sense and not, as the judge says at the beginning, a woman whose "contempt for all religious principle and social obligation threatens to undermine the whole fabric of our civilization." She sells her life story to the newspapers to pay for Gulley's and Tommy's bills until she will be free to work again. And though she promises to better herself and "keep a more watchful eye, next time, on my flesh, now I know better," she is unrepentant because she is a free soul; a modern Eve, she falls into freedom; a free woman, she poses the problem of a natural morality for which she is condemned. The remaining two novels of the trilogy complete the portrait of Sara.

Structurally, *Herself Surprised* is enclosed by the trial of Sara for theft; it ends where it began, with her being sentenced to prison. She looks back on her life, seeing it in the perspective of the human relationships she has created with others—Matt Monday, Gulley Jimson, Tom Wilcher. *To Be a Pilgrim* begins where *Herself Surprised* leaves off, with Sara in prison, and it ends with Sara just out of prison nearly eighteen months later. Tom Wilcher, looking back on his life, seeing it in the perspective of history and morality, interprets the meaning of his relationship with Sara; to him Sara is the saver of lost souls. Sara is too much the innocent to know the full significance of her life; she is too busy living and creating life to reflect on it except to wonder at herself surprised. *The Horse's Mouth* completes the portrait of Sara begun in *Herself Surprised* and developed in *To Be a Pilgrim*. It begins about where *To Be a Pilgrim* left off, showing Sara's life from the time when, out of prison, she attempts to build a new relationship with Mr. Byles, to her death as the result of Gulley's attack. Through Gulley's eyes we see her as the female principle, the undying Eve, a force of nature, the life of the body itself, with which he as man and artist is constantly at war. Her act of forgiveness at the end frees Gulley and is her own salvation.

Originally, we were to see Gulley as the artist and Wilcher as the historian of the past through Sara's eyes. While Sara does comment on Gulley and Wilcher in *Herself Surprised*, her commentary is limited by her essential female approach to relationships and by her unreflectiveness. Cary eliminated much of Sara's commentary and reflections on art and history in order to remain "true" to her essential character. One deleted scene is especially interesting because it brings all three protagonists together. This scene corresponds to Chapter 65 of the published text, but whereas in the published version Sara merely reports second hand the information that Gulley and Wilcher met and talked cordially about art, the original version has Sara present during part of a rather uncordial argument about art:

He [Wilcher] shook hands with Jimison and gave him a bow as he always did and said "I have herad [sic] the name, of course; you are one of the modern school, Mr. Jimison, are you not?" and he began to talk art and to say that, for his part, his tastes were old fashioned.

"So are mine" Jimison said, as cool as you please "give me Greco or Blake—the only good art is religious art."

"Quite so—quite so—Mr. W. said delighted, the only question is what is religious art. For instance, you speak of Blake—"

"One of the most religious men who ever lived" Gulley said.

"An an[a]rchist. Come, Mr. Jimison, anarchy is not a religion. By definition, religion is bringing together—it requires some kind of system—some agreement or creed."

"Blake had a very strong faith," Gulley said, getting warm.[12]

When Sara leaves, Wilcher, the master of the house, opens the door for her. Although she is his housekeeper, "It was one of the little things which he did without thinking, because of his good breeding," [13] in contrast to Gulley who had just punched her on the nose. Later, after Gulley has left, Wilcher comments to Sara:

"Mr. Jimison is a very interesting man—but if you will excuse me, I thought him a little headstrong. It was not that his opinions are different from jine [sic]—I enjoy a good discussion—but that he seemed to think his ideas were the only possible ones."
So I said only that I had never understood Jimison's religion.[14]

In the continuation of the same scene Sara comments on Wilcher's respect for women:

When I knew Mr. W better I knew he was a man who never blamed women for anything except adultery or disloyalty or lying or cruelty. In his mind, women were truly made for service; not of men, he would say, but of god and of god's family; and they were subject to god's law and so, by his order, to the head of their families, which was a man.[15]

Wilcher's conservatism and traditionalism are shown in terms of religion and the family. In contrast, Gulley's anarchism and godlike creativity are revealed in another rejected commentary by Sara:

He hated all governments, not because of the laws against adultery, but because he truly thought that they bring evil into the world, with msery [sic] and laws. Of god too he spoke with great love and earnestness, saying why had flowers been made beautiful to us if god in them did not make beauty and god in us did not feel the beauty he had made. I used to smile, when he spoke so, in the middle hours of the night, that he would paint the beauty he loved instead of his green men and fat women, but I did not say so then, on our honeymoon, and all among our happiness.[16]

Another canceled passage in the final typescript of *Herself Surprised* illustrates Cary's decision to keep the force of Sara's essential character by cutting out reflective commentary. In this particular passage Sara reflects on her own attitude toward religion:

I know people laugh at the devil now and say there is no such person, but if it is God in our hearts who tries to make us do good, then what is it in our bodies and minds, always tempting us to do evil. The old squire at my home who was the vicar too, used to say that it was easier to believe in the devil than God for everyone knew the promptings of evil but some never had a good thought. Now in this place of just punishment, I remember this every hour, though you may say I am only a foolish old woman, who never had much education; still I have come back to that old belief. I am driven to it.[17]

The cuts that Cary made in the manuscript of *Herself Surprised* were necessitated by his rule "character first," but they do not weaken the portraits of Tom Wilcher and Gulley Jimson who speak for themselves. Though the original scheme for the trilogy had to be modified because of the cuts, the trilogy itself is not fundamentally weakened, for the "essential Sara" is central to the lives of Jimson and Wilcher. To have diluted the quality and force of Sara's character would have been to lose, or at least weaken, the central meaning of her life as it affected Wilcher and Jimson—the element of grace and the everlasting Eve. The portrait of Sara is made three-dimensional by the commentary of Tom Wilcher and Gulley Jimson in *To Be a Pilgrim* and *The Horse's Mouth;* the portraits of Wilcher and Jimson are made three-dimensional not so much by what Sara says of them, but by the dimension she adds to their lives and by their articulate understanding of her.

TO BE A PILGRIM (1942)

Though *To Be a Pilgrim* is closely related in narrative time to *Herself Surprised*, beginning at about the point

where the first novel ends, it is not as closely related in
character and tone. Gulley Jimson does not appear at all
in this second novel; although she is part of Tom Wilcher's memory, Sara is a late addition, and she appears
only in one scene, being in prison during most of the
novel. Yet *To Be a Pilgrim* as the middle novel of the
trilogy gives coherence to the whole; its theme adds a
moral and historical dimension to the lives of Sara and
Gulley through the voice of Tom Wilcher. Sara is too
unreflective and inarticulate to be an interpretative observer. Gulley Jimson is too much the egoistic artist to be
the historian of the past. It is Tom Wilcher, introspective and religious, who interprets the past as a pilgrim's progress and thus gives meaning to the present
lives of the other characters and his own.

To be a pilgrim is to live a meaningful purposeful life,
to know where one is going, which presumes a starting
point—the heritage of the past—as well as a goal. "A pilgrim is not a lost soul, I thought, nor a wanderer. He is
not a tramp," [18] Tom Wilcher says, for "what is faith but
the belief that in life there is something worth doing, and
the feeling of it?" (page 35). Tom Wilcher is a pilgrim;
his moral conscience is the continuity of England's Protestant heritage and his sense of the past is the continuity
of England's democratic tradition unbroken by changes
in appearance. Underneath the changing exterior of
moral codes, political revolutions, economic and social
upheavals, he is the steady undercurrent of tradition and
order that asks where are we going, to what purpose,
why. He is the heritage of Protestant liberalism that can
be shocked by his brother Edward's duplicity and cynicism as a practicing politician (the prototype of Chester
Nimmo, the protagonist of the second trilogy). He is the
heritage of eighteenth-century rationalism that can be
repelled by his sister Lucy's religious fanaticism. He is the
heritage of Anglican morality that can still be shocked,
not by the fact of Ann's extramarital relations with Robert, but by her cold, clinical attitude. He is the heritage

of the past that resists change and yet must bow to it inevitably, not because he is stuffy and old-fashioned as the younger generation would like to see him, but because he questions the sense of destroying all of the past—the good with the bad—merely for the sake of being different.

All this—his sense of duty, his love of order, his conservative desire to preserve the values of the past, his love of Tolbrook with its deep roots in the past—makes Tom Wilcher the direct opposite of Gulley Jimson who as creator must be the destroyer of the past. Cary notes that Wilcher "hates enemies of the loved order. Destruction, violence, meanness, dis-grace, war, spite, disorder, extravagance." And indeed, their brief encounter in *The Horse's Mouth* is one of mutual dislike and enmity. But what links them together is the attraction of opposites: both are pilgrims, for they know where they are going; they are not lost souls. If Tom Wilcher had really known Gulley Jimson, he would approve of him, as he did of Sara, not as a person, definitely not as an artist, but as a pilgrim believing in himself, journeying to the promised land of fulfillment though never reaching it because always there is something more wonderful and beautiful beyond the horizon. Wilcher's quarrel is not with change, but with lack of purpose and direction. "The *essence of life is in the creative change*," [19] Cary writes in an unpublished note. Wilcher hopes to start a new life with Sara, to be a pilgrim creating a new world away from Tolbrook and the past, and though he is prevented from realizing his pilgrimage by his relatives and by his own divided soul, he understands through Sara the pilgrim's mind.

If Sara is the unchanging Eve creating "a society, a relationship, a spiritual world" for herself and her man, and Gulley is the unchanging Adam, doubting, developing, evolving, destroying that which he has created in order to envision a larger creation, then Tom Wilcher is the unchanging pilgrim in the land of unfulfilled promise.

He is the divided soul "living the past, and yet acknowl-
edging the rights of the future, *and the need for change*
for the pilgrimage"; he is burdened by his sense of duty
and responsibility which binds him to the past and limits
his freedom, but paradoxically he is freed by his faith,
which in its living form, Cary writes, is "always the same
faith but with a different expression. Like an art it can
never repeat itself"; it is a creative act of the soul "to be
a pilgrim of God." [20]

To Be a Pilgrim begins:

> Last month I suffered a great misfortune in the loss of my
> housekeeper, Mrs. Jimson. She was sent to prison for pawning
> some old trinkets which I had long forgotten. My relatives
> discovered the fact and called in the police before I could
> intervene. They knew I fully intended, as I still intend, to
> marry Sara Jimson. They were good people. They saw me as
> a foolish old man, who had fallen into the hands of a scheming
> woman. But they were quite wrong. It was I who was the
> unfaithful servant, and Sara the victim. It was because I did
> not give Sara enough pay and because she did not like to ask
> me for money that she ran into debt, and was tempted to take
> some useless trifles from the attic [page 9].

Much of this first paragraph sets the theme of the novel
and relates it to the other two novels of the trilogy.
Sara, as we saw in *Herself Surprised*, was right in believing
that Tom Wilcher would never miss the things she stole
and that he would understand and forgive her. The relatives are unforgiving and threaten to have Wilcher declared insane if he does not give up his intention of
marrying her. Wilcher never gets to marry Sara; it is
evident that his plan to marry her is only a gesture, a
hold on the future which is no longer his to decide. He
is a dying man, he belongs to the past which is being
destroyed, he is the spokesman for a generation that is
dying.

The relatives, who represent the new generation, are
positive and righteous in their judgment that Sara has
schemed to cheat a doting old man out of his wealth

and that her theft is proof of her criminal intentions. They want to inherit Tolbrook Farm and Tom Wilcher's money when he dies; it is, they believe, their just due for being born Wilchers, the lawmakers and rulers of the nation, and not Sara Mondays, the kitchen maids and housekeepers. None of them would say with Tom Wilcher: "It was I who was the unfaithful servant, and Sara the victim."

Tom Wilcher is of the same generation as Gulley Jimson, but he seems old by comparison. Partly this is the result of his being pitted against the younger generation and the change that they represent, particularly against Ann Wilcher and Robert Brown, his niece and nephew. Partly it is the result of his belonging to the past, re-creating it in his memory (even at times mistaking it for the present) and revealing its significance and purpose. He is the spokesman for his generation, stating the pilgrim's faith in the future of his country: England "the wandering Dutchman, the pilgrim and scapegoat of the world" will survive the coming war because she is free and "stands always before all possibility, and that is the youth of the spirit" (page 342). What is needed is faith, "the belief that in life there is something worth doing."

Sara gave him faith, and Tolbrook Farm with its deep roots in the past is the object of his faith. Like E. M. Forster's *Howard's End*, Tolbrook Farm is a symbol of England, and as in Forster's novel the question of who inherits the land becomes the question who shall inherit England.[21] The original plan for *To Be a Pilgrim*, as revealed in Cary's unpublished notes, was to have Wilcher set fire to Tolbrook in order to escape his responsibilities (and collect the insurance money) and be free to live with Sara; but because of the arson no insurance is payable, and he is financially ruined. Instead of the freedom he sought, he is sent to the asylum, where he is content because he no longer has property or responsibility.[22] An alternative plan was to have Wilcher involved in a crime to which he confesses; he is arrested, Sara

gives evidence against him, and he is jailed and dies in
jail. Before he is arrested, he "goes to say goodbye to
house, tells story of each room, the pond, deaths, his
sister's life etc." [23]

Both plans were rejected, but Cary retained elements
that suggested possibilities to him. In the final version
Wilcher "confesses" to Blanche that he "might set the
place on fire as I did to Craven Gardens" (page 133).
Faulty wiring may have started the fire, but he had discovered it and could have stopped it: "I may even have
assisted it to burn" (page 134), he says. The truth is left
ambiguous. Also, he was in trouble with the police because he accosted young girls; he was not arrested, but
the police warned his family, and they, in turn, threatened to shut him up in an asylum (pages 308-11). Cary
uses this material, suggested by the alternative original
plan of the novel, to show the depths of Wilcher's despair
and loneliness after the death of his sister Lucy and his
rejection by Julie, some time before Sara became his
housekeeper. It is Sara who rescued him from his corruption (which is reflected in the corruption of nations
"walking on the very edge of war and destruction" [page
311]). Out of despair, new faith was born, and Sara
"came to save my soul alive" by giving him happiness
and renewing his faith.

To have Wilcher burn down Tolbrook or to end his
life in jail as a criminal would have vitiated much of the
significance of Tolbrook as a symbol, and it would also
have weakened Wilcher's role as the spokesman of his
generation and made the basic theme of the novel, a pilgrim's faith, ambiguous if not impossible. Wilcher is no
saint in the final version, but neither is he a sinner whose
soul is damned: as the pilgrim he hears God's cry to men,
"Break all, die all, that ye be born again." Though Cary
does not have Wilcher confess to a crime and then say
goodbye to Tolbrook, he does retain the revelation of
the living past haunting the rooms of the house. He alter-
nates the past and present so that the past becomes a

living part of present history and experience; the past gives meaning to the present and the present gives understanding to the past, a technique he uses again in *The Moonlight*.

Tolbrook is a structural symbol more closely resembling the lighthouse symbol in Virginia Woolf's *To the Lighthouse* than the more incidental symbol in Forster's *Howard's End*. Like the lighthouse, it is the central focus of the novel, enclosing its formal structure and infusing its internal structure. Like the lighthouse, it is a complex symbol illuminating the theme of the novel and meaning different things to the characters, both present and past.

To Tom Wilcher, Tolbrook is a dual symbol of love and hate, and because of this duality his attitude is at first ambivalent. It represents in the present his imprisonment away from Sara; his immediate plan is to escape Tolbrook, its responsibilities and its connections with the past, when the time comes to marry Sara. Thus his hope of freedom and a future pilgrimage with Sara lies entirely outside Tolbrook. When he does "escape" to London to see Sara, his effort is futile; Sara, who has already made a new life for herself with Fred, betrays Wilcher by wiring Robert and Ann to take him back to Tolbrook. He cannot escape Tolbrook any more than he can escape his death. He goes home to die.

He fears the house, for he fears the hold it has on him. Tolbrook is the past, his past and England's; its rooms are alive with the voices of the past, its furniture and familiar objects are peopled with memories. As the past unfolds, evoked in his memory by the house, we see not only his personal past and that of his family—the religious zeal of Lucy, the political career of Edward, the soldiery of Bill and the stability of Amy—but also the history of England from the 1880's to 1939 as it is lived by the Wilcher family. His past was a conflict of love and duty (as his present is a conflict of his love for Sara and his sense of duty toward the past and Tolbrook). As

Cary writes in a note, Wilcher "adores Lucy but she loves Edward & always sacrifices him to Edward. Both condescend to him while he serves them." [24] His sense of duty caused him to sacrifice his love for Julie until it was too late to find happiness. He found himself a parasite on the creative lives of others while he had no purpose of his own. It is the women—Lucy, Amy, and later Sara and Ann—who, through love, make his life and Tolbrook purposeful.

To Robert Brown, Lucy's son, Tolbrook is a farm to be run, a practical proposition. The changes he makes are necessary to modernize the farm. The past represented by the grove of trees and the drawing room is already dead and must make way for the new. Wilcher cannot stop Robert from destroying the past; he cannot stop change. But he can interpret the symbolic significance of Tolbrook:

But he [Robert] does not destroy Tolbrook, he takes it back into history, which changed it once before from priory into farm, from farm into manor. . . . Robert has brought it back into the English stream and he himself has come with it; to the soft corn, good for home-made bread; the mixed farm, so good for men, to the old church religion which is so twined with English life, that the very prayers seem to breathe of fields after rain and skies whose light is falling between clouds.[25]

To Blanche Wilcher, married to Bill's son, Tolbrook is an inheritance out of which she will not be cheated by a scheming housekeeper, even if she has to have her uncle declared insane. She has the best claim to Tolbrook but the least interest in it. Ann Wilcher, Edward's daughter, on the other hand, though she is at first indifferent to Tolbrook, comes to love it as she lives there, perceiving some of Tom Wilcher's feeling and sharing her husband's need for it. All three—Blanche, Ann, and Robert —inherit Tolbrook. All three, for better or worse, inherit England. Tom Wilcher, having spoken for his generation, is ready to die and let the younger generation take over.

The world of Tolbrook is an enclosed world, and structurally it encloses the novel, as Sara's imprisonment encloses *Herself Surprised*. Wilcher will die at Tolbrook, a prisoner of the past who discovers as he relives the past that all along he was the keeper of the keys:

> I never liked lodgings. I was too fond of my dear ones at home. And what if they were trees and chairs and furniture and books and stones?
> Material love. What is material? What is body? Is not this house the house of spirits, made by generations of lovers? I touched in my mother the warmth of a love that did not belong to either of us. Why should I not feel, when I lie in English ground, the passion of a spirit that beats in all English souls [page 342].

Both Gulley Jimson and Sara Monday are free because they are creative while Tom Wilcher is the captive of the past. But, Cary notes, "Freedom, as creation" must be "guarded by *wisdom*." [26]

THE HORSE'S MOUTH (1944)

The Horse's Mouth is as different in style and tone from *To Be a Pilgrim* as Gulley Jimson and Tom Wilcher are different in temperament and outlook. From the very first paragraph the novel is permeated with Gulley's teeming creative mind:

> I was walking by the Thames. Half-past morning on an autumn day. Sun in a mist. Like an orange in a fried fish shop. All bright below. Low tide, dusty water and a crooked bar of straw, chicken-boxes, dirt and oil from mud to mud. Like a viper swimming in skim milk. The old serpent, symbol of nature and love.[27]

The staccato phrases take the reader into the imagination of the artist at the moment of creation. The artist's eye has created from reality the startling, antiromantic detail of the sun looking like an orange in a fried fish shop. The flow of free association, the main device of the stream of consciousness technique, is used in the second image: the Thames, at low tide, looks like a viper swimming in skim milk; the viper calls to mind the old serpent symbol, and by direct association recalls Blake and the first of the many quotations in the novel:

> Five windows light the caverned man; through one
>   he breathes the air
> Through one hears music of the spheres; through
>   one can look
> And see small portions of the eternal world.[28]

Like all of the quotations in the novel this one is relevant to the content. Gulley is fond of quoting Blake because like Blake he is a rebel and like Blake he seeks to paint the symbolic creation and fall of man; but it is not made merely to remind the reader of the similarities between Blake and Gulley. As Cary states in an unpublished note, "Point of Blake is his depth and adequacy—close to the ground. His acceptance of *evil as real.* Through creation, generation to regeneration. The stoic english view but he *enters into freedom and individuality* through experience." [29]

This first quotation is significant on many levels. Gulley has just been released from prison; he is free to paint, but in another sense he is not free to paint because he is unable to buy paints and canvas. He is forced to borrow from friends, swindle strangers, steal from paint-store owners, and use old canvases in order to be free to paint. Freedom is necessary for the artist; the artist is freed by the act of creation, but he must be free to create, which brings up the whole question of Gulley's poverty.

Gulley Jimson paints because he is creative, not because he wants fame, success, money. He is the artist forever at odds with society. He could make money by repeating his earlier style, now that the public has caught up with Impressionism, but it would be repetition, not creation. Whether he is successful or not by society's standards does not matter to him, nor does it matter whether posterity might eventually appreciate his earlier style; he has gone on to something else. Society owes him a living because he is the creator. But instead it hounds him and puts him in jail. It will not support his art; it fears the rebel, as it feared William Blake. Society expects Gulley to conform to its taste, and then it will buy his paintings, but to do so would be the death of him as an artist. And the death of the artist, the creator, is the death of society, for it is through the vision of the artist that society is taught new ways of seeing.

Cary's theme—the conflict of the artist and society in the modern world—poses the paradox of injustice and freedom. Society has not fulfilled its obligation to the creative genius since the aristocratic patron left the scene centuries ago; its academies and national galleries support the dead academician, not the living creator; its universities and colleges support the parasitic critic, not the writer; its middle class, the arbiters of taste, support their comfortable image of Ruskin's beauty and laugh at new art with the same laugh that greeted the post-Impressionist exhibition at the Grafton Gallery in London in 1910. This is the element of injustice in the world, the price the artist pays for his freedom to create: *"Injustice* as necessary element of chance. Freedom as creation, & power of mind. i.e. one must create and this is the joy." [30]

Paradoxically, art is a prison for the artist; he is bound by the limitations of his form, his subject matter, his technique. His eyes "can look and see small portions of the eternal world," but not the whole; though the five senses are windows, man is caverned in his body. Those who would condemn and imprison Gulley for his irresponsible behavior have not half the discipline of mind and body. It is this very discipline which gives him the fullest freedom and purpose in life—the freedom of the imagination (at the very moment of his escape from the

owner of the paint shop from whom Gulley has "bor-
rowed" a few cans of paint, his imagination is at work on
his painting of "The Fall," left uncompleted when he was
sent to prison).

The body is a prison for Gulley as a man, betraying the
artist in him: "Gulley feeling betrayed by his hands and
legs [i.e., treachery of the body]. Got to *create* a point
of view—but even then the body does you down," [31] Cary
states in a note. Gulley, a dying old man, feels the desperation of time, now that he is "free" from prison: "And I
perceived that I hadn't time to waste on pleasure. A man
of my age has to get on with the job" (page 11). He takes
desperate action to "get on with the job," but he must
"waste" his time trying to borrow or steal money to pay
for artist's supplies and a place to paint. He knows there is
little time left to accomplish all that he has to do. He suffers from high blood pressure and must control his anger
against the injustice of the world. Thus, he constantly reminds himself "not to get into a state." He wears a comic
mask and treats everything as a joke, for if he were to let
himself "get into a state" over the tragedy of the artist in
the modern world, it would kill him.

The first-person narrative method of *The Horse's
Mouth* not only reveals the mind of the artist, but also illuminates the tragedy of the creative mind: the comic
mask which Gulley wears intensifies the catastrophe at
the end. Were it not for this method we would see mainly
the comedy of action, the impudence and irreverence of
the character. Instead we also see the artist at work. *The
Horse's Mouth* is, as Cary says, "A study of the creative
imagination working in symbols." [32]

The comedy is Gulley's struggle with society; the tragedy is Gulley's struggle with himself and his art. To
Gulley "society" is law, authority, popular taste, the
Boorjays, and thus to be defied because the artist must be
free. Even art itself becomes hardened into a style and is
to be rebelled against. To society Gulley is the bohemian
exile, the *avant garde* artist, the immoral and irresponsible

man (Gulley does steal, cheat, and lie, but basically it is to get money so that he can go on painting, and he is honest with himself when it comes to matters of art). What then becomes clear is the tragic implications of the artist's struggle to release the creative vision from the prison within himself and translate it into the discipline of form and technique.

This struggle is parodied on the comic level by Gulley's quarrel with society. But even the comic reveals the tragedy of the artist in the modern world: the artist is not valued by society; it fears him as a creator, hates him as a rebel, envies him as a free man. Both the comic and the tragic come to a climax in the final scene. Authority has finally caught up with Gulley (but the police are not there to arrest him for the death of Sara, only to get him away from the building which is to be demolished); time has caught up with him (the wall collapses on him); life has caught up with him (he has had a stroke and is dying). He cannot finish his monumental painting of The Creation, for creation is never complete; art is never at a standstill, and the creative imagination of the artist is never satisfied. That is both the triumph and the defeat of the artist: Gulley says to the nun in the hospital at the end, " 'I should laugh all round my neck at this minute if my shirt wasn't a bit on the tight side.' 'It would be better for you to pray.' 'Same thing, mother' " (page 297). The comic and the tragic merge.

The structure of *The Horse's Mouth* arises out of the thematic relationship of Gulley's paintings to the quotations from Blake. The three major paintings—"The Fall," "The Raising of Lazarus," and "The Creation"—are the structural foci of the novel; the passages from Blake (and Gulley's commentary on them) interpret the symbolic content of the paintings and reveal the organic relationship of the paintings to the theme. The paintings are interrelated thematically, developing the theme of freedom.

Although two thirds of the novel is devoted to the first painting, "The Fall," there are three different but related efforts by Gulley to put on canvas his changing concept of paradise lost. The first effort antedates the opening of the novel; it was left uncompleted while Gulley served his prison sentence, and was entitled "The Living God," a symbolic representation of the temptation of Adam and Eve. The living god is the Blakean serpent, symbol of nature and love. The canvas has been ruined in his absence —it has been shot with an air gun, a piece a foot square has been cut out of Adam's middle, and names have been written all over Eve. Nosy Barbon is indignant, but Gulley is on the surface remarkably calm and facetious. The calm, comic attitude masks the serious conflict of the artist with the philistines. His poverty, the delay in getting on with the job when he is desperate for time, the injustices of the world are all intensified by this seeming catastrophe. It is not a catastrophe, however, because Gulley's imagination is at work seeing how the painting can be completed, rearranging the shapes and changing the colors. He discovers that the canvas can be patched and to replace his supplies, which have been stolen, he steals paint and makes a brush out of a piece of rope.

In this second attempt to paint "The Fall," Adam gives Gulley no trouble (for he is Adam, the male principle), but Eve is a problem. When he goes with Coker to visit Sara his thoughts are about Eve and The Fall: "Through generation to generation. The door of paradise. This way to the Holy land. Fall to rise again" (page 41). He quotes phrases from Blake: "For everything that lives is holy. Life delights in life." Paradise is lost but life is gained. He then quotes from Blake's "Milton":

> For every generated body in its inward form
> Is a garden of delight and a building of magnificence
> Built by the sons of Los
> And the herbs and flowers and furniture and beds and
> chambers
> Continually woven in the looms of Enitharmon's daughters.
> In bright cathedrons golden domes with care and love and
> tears [page 41].

Gulley's irreverent interpretation of this passage—"That is to say, old Billy Blake dreamed dreams while Mrs. Blake emptied the pot"—reveals his concept of The Fall as a division into male and female principle, the male creating new dreams and the female creating a domestic society for herself and her man.

To Gulley, Sara is the female principle, the modern Eve: "I was thinking that Sara at about forty had been just what I wanted for my Eve. That falls every night to rise in the morning. And wonder at herself. Knowing everything and still surprised. Living in innocence" (pages 41-42). Gulley's attitude toward Sara, the living Eve, is ambivalent. She inspires him as an artist: "Yes, I thought, all alivoh. Eve should be a woman of forty with five children and grey hairs coming, trying on a new velvet. Looking at herself in the glass, as if she's never seen herself before" (page 42). But his personal relationship with her interferes with his artistic freedom; he is afraid of Sara's "care and love and tears," which enslave him to her sexuality and materiality: "It was, 'Poor Gulley, don't forget your cough medicine. Now darling, what about your socks. I'm sure they're wet.' And when I was mad to paint, she was for putting me to bed and getting in after me" (pages 51-52). Quoting Blake, he states the duality of body and spirit, man and God, as symbolized by the Christ image in "The Mental Traveller": the spirit is bound by materiality and yet the prophetic vision arises out of nature. Gulley's remedy for Sara's maternal instincts is to punch her on the nose: "Materiality, that is, Sara, the old female nature, having attempted to button up the prophetic spirit, that is to say, Gulley Jimson, in her placket-hole, got a bonk on the conk, and was reduced to her proper status, as spiritual fodder" (page 52).

Sexuality and creativity are linked as in Joyce and Lawrence, but without Stephen Dedalus' ordination into the priesthood of art or Paul Morel's agony of the flesh: "even when I was having the old girl, I was getting after some ideal composition in my head. Taking advantage of the general speed up of the clockwork" (pages 52–53). Sara, as a woman, and thus as nature, is as necessary to Gulley's art as his paints, brushes, and canvases. The artist must go to nature for his forms, shapes, lines, colors; he is free, he is creative, when he uses the material of nature to compose some ideal composition: he "binds her down for his delight . . . And she becomes his dwelling-place / And garden fruitful seventy fold." [33] The artist is the prisoner of his art form as the soul is the prisoner of the body, struggling against material limitations to release the spiritual vision.

Sara is only one aspect of Gulley's struggle for freedom. If Sara "lives upon his shrieks and cries," then the critic "nails him down upon a rock / Catches his shrieks in cups of gold": "Which means," Gulley interprets, "that some old woman of a blue nose nails your work of imagination to the rock of law, and why and what; and submits him to a logical analysis" (page 48). The critic, like Sara, attempts to "button up the prophetic spirit," label it and shelve it; he is not free because he is not creative, but he can make or break an artist's reputation as an arbiter of taste. The rich art patron (represented by Hickson and Beeder) is one step further removed from freedom because he depends on the critic's analysis, but he can also make or break an artist's reputation by buying or not buying his paintings. Styles in painting change as new revolutions in art occur—Gulley's father is left behind by the revolution in art in the 1860's; Gulley himself goes through the whole range of modern styles. The artist must destroy old forms to create new ones; to be free to create he must destroy the old vision, for repetition is not creative. Art must die to be reborn.

The third and final attempt by Gulley to complete his painting on the subject of The Fall explicitly states the theme of this first section—the fall into freedom. Sara is central to this theme: Sara, the everlasting Eve, is identified with Blake's Oothoon, the everlasting maiden, "the eternal innocence that thinks no evil" (page 104).

The portrait of Sara begun in *Herself Surprised* is completed in *The Horse's Mouth:* hers is the surprise of innocence in every fall. Gulley's ambivalence toward Sara is resolved because as artist he is freed from Sara the individual woman tempting him as she becomes Oothoon-Eve, a symbol of all womankind to the artist. The Sara of the bath painting is the personal impression of the artist Gulley; the Sara of "The Fall" is to be the impersonal force of nature symbolizing regeneration. Sara's Gulley becomes Blake's Adam, the symbol of "imagination born of love. . . . The fall into manhood, into responsibility, into sin. Into freedom. Into wisdom" (pages 118-19). The Fall into freedom is the Blakean fall "into the real world among the everlasting forms, the solid" (page 174).

Before Gulley can translate these ideas onto canvas he suffers a double catastrophe: he is sent to prison for stealing from Hickson, and six months later, when he is free again, he discovers that Coker's mother has cut up his canvas to patch the leaking roof. But at the very moment of tragedy Gulley laughs and celebrates himself as creator. The uses of beauty are many but limited; the creation of beauty is infinite and boundless. The main theme of the novel is revealed at this point: the artist as creator is God—"I have transformed a chunk of wood, canvas, etc., into a spiritual fact, an eternal beauty. I am God." [34] He can create a new Fall or raise Lazarus from the dead.

"The Raising of Lazarus," Gulley's second painting, recapitulates and completes the theme of *To Be a Pilgrim* as "The Fall" rounds out the meaning of *Herself Surprised*. Just before Gulley goes to Sir William Beeder's apartment, where he appropriates the wall for his painting of Lazarus, he meets Tom Wilcher coming out of Sara's house. His dislike of Wilcher is as strong as Wilcher's dislike of him. Their mutual antagonism is partly that of one Adam to another in rivalry over the same Eve. But the antagonism is also symbolic: "Abstract philosophy warring in enmity against Imagination" (page 186), Gulley quotes Blake. The rational man is the enemy of the imaginative man. The man of imagination takes his forms from the real world "composed of individual creatures, fields and moons and trees and stars and cats and flowers and women and sauce-pans and bicycles and men" (page 186). The man of reason abstracts and categorizes: "You're a Lost Soul, or a Bad Husband, or a Modern Artist, or a Good Citizen, or a Suspicious Character, or an Income Tax Payer" (page 186). To Wilcher, Gulley is a Modern Artist and therefore a thoroughly immoral man and an example of what's wrong with the modern world (one must note also that Gulley categorizes Wilcher and therefore is incapable of understanding him as an individual human being). To Gulley, Wilcher is a "blackcoat man with the fires of death and hell burning under him, a phantom, a spectre living in a spectral world of abstractions, a black scorpion ringed with hellfire, a demon" (pages 185–86). He is a Lazarus raised from the dead, the Lost Soul saved by Sara's love.

Gulley's painting of Lazarus on the wall of the Beeders' apartment is the central focus of the most comic scene in the novel (pages 195–214). Gulley's irreverent attitude toward Sir Beeder's property, toward the old masters hanging on the wall, toward art itself, is the antithesis of Wilcher's traditionalism and conservatism. His comic exuberance and Godlike egoism is the antithesis of Wilcher's seriousness and humility. Gulley is the creator, Wilcher the servant of God. Wilcher is the lost soul resurrected, but Gulley is the artist resurrecting life.

Before Gulley can complete his painting of Lazarus, the Beeders return, and he makes his escape. The resurrection theme is inverted: Gulley escapes the law (government), but he forgives government for what it does; "it can't rise out of its damnation" because it has no imagination. Lazarus cannot rise out of his damnation by himself; only Blake's Satan, the man of imagination, through the marriage of heaven and hell, and Blake's

Christ, lamb and tiger, resurrect themselves. The artist as the man of imagination and as Godlike creator resurrects himself. Gulley, banished from lawful society, without any prospects of doing another painting, is brought back to life again by his imagination which seizes upon the materials of nature and creates a new world:

I hadn't seen a real wild tree for twelve years. I couldn't take my eyes off 'em, bulging out into the moon as solid as whales. By God, I thought, no one has seen a tree till this moment. And I believe I could paint it. And then again I felt that shape of the big fish and Churchill's hat. I felt an idea, a big one [page 222].

This is the seminal idea for his final painting, "The Creation."

The subject of "The Creation" is the final development of the theme of freedom as creation and the celebration of Gulley Jimson the creator. The Adam and Eve theme of the fall into freedom with its regeneration through love and the resurrection theme of rebirth through faith are the symbolic elements of creation. The center of creation is God, "the old 'un who dreams it all for the first time." [35] God is the dreamer, the imagination, and Adam is Godlike, for he is the man of imagination. The painting itself is a creation of The Creation, and Gulley-Adam is its creator.

Eve becomes the woman-tree "with something of Lolie about the roots"; Sara becomes an impersonalized symbol of The Fall into freedom, merging with all women into the essential woman. She reappears symbolically as the she-whale nursing her calf. The fish, the primitive and Christian symbol of regeneration, is linked with the resurrection theme in the form of the she-whale, represented in the painting with a woman's head. Sara, as the symbol of nature, the female principle, is the paradoxical death and life of the soul. As Eve, the temptress of Adam, she destroys the original paradise, but by her fall freedom is created and new life is generated. The fall into freedom is the possibility of infinite creation. As the she-whale, the predatory female principle, she swallows Jonah, but through her love resurrects the lost soul, Wilcher, a new man reborn with faith, like Jonah.

The whale symbol is complex because it is linked with classical and primitive mythology. In the painting the she-whale rests on the broken edge of "the cave of eternal rock" while she nurses her calf. The classical myth of man's descent into the underworld (death) so that his soul may be reborn is related to the Christian myths of Jonah and the whale, Lazarus raised from the dead and Christ's resurrection, all of which in Gulley's painting are represented by the figure of the she-whale resting on the edge of the cave.

Orpheus' descent into the underworld is implicitly related to Gulley the artist who, like Orpheus, is immortal through his art. The cave and the fish, primitive symbols of fertility and rebirth, are linked together in the painting. The womb is the source of regeneration of life, but it also symbolically represents the artist's need to renew himself through nature, the source of his creativity. Zeus, as both male and female principle, could create life himself. God, as the one "who dreams it all for the first time," could create both Adam and Eve. Gulley, as artist, can imagine Adam and Eve and create "The Creation," but as an Adam he must gain and renew his freedom through an Eve; whether it is a woman, a tree, or a fish he must take his forms and colors from nature.

Though Gulley frees himself from Sara through his imagination and his art, he is not free of her as a human being; it is Sara, instead, who frees him that he might continue to create. Gulley returns to Sara in the hope of getting money for his new idea, "The Creation." There is a suggestion of the Orpheus-Eurydice myth in his return: for a moment they are reunited, but when she screams for the police because Gulley is stealing her painting (the painting he created), he hits her over the head and pushes her away from the window to silence her; to be caught by the police would be the death of him, the end of his idea for the new painting. Accidentally, Sara "fell down the cellar stairs into some dark hole" (page 263). Gulley escapes, leaving Sara behind in the underworld to die. Sara saves Gulley from the police (death) by giving them a wrong description; she frees him (rebirth) so that he might be free to create. By her act of grace she forgives him and sets him free, new-born into life, as his mother did giving birth to him, recreating the creator, Blake's "little creature born of joy and mirth" (with old Mother Groper, an old tart and the village midwife as the angel presiding at His birth). "Go love," his mother had said in Blake's words, "without the help of anything on earth" (page 263). Birth is a fall into freedom. "And that's real horse meat," for it is straight from the horse's mouth. To fall is to discover one's self.

Gulley never completes his painting, but creation is never complete. Life and art, Cary is saying, both stand before all possibilities. Creation is infinite; beauty unlimited in its variety. Gulley's life is completed, but art and life go on. To laugh is the same as to pray, Gulley says at the end. He has made a joke of life, Cary says in the preface, "because he dare not take it seriously." The comic mask hides his rage at the injustices in the world and the enemies of his freedom; yet the comic mask reveals the true source of his religious feeling, the joy of creation.

As the final novel of the trilogy Cary used *The Horse's Mouth* to extend the meaning of the first two novels and complete the portrait of Gulley Jimson, an artist's self-portrait. Both Wilcher and Jimson complete the portrait of Sara; they see her from different points of view, but together they fill in the missing pieces. Wilcher reveals the human side of Sara, against which Gulley constantly wars; Gulley reveals the aesthetic side of Sara through his art, which Wilcher does not know. Wilcher interprets the past since both Sara and Gulley live entirely for the present. Gulley interprets the present through his art because his art creates the present. Sara sees herself, for neither Wilcher nor Gulley can reveal the whole Sara. Wilcher speaks for himself because neither Sara, who is unreflective, nor Gulley, who is his enemy, can speak for him. Gulley speaks for himself because neither Sara nor Wilcher can speak for the artist.

The Horse's Mouth by recapitulating the meaning of the first two novels in the first two paintings and stating its own theme in the third painting reveals in its structure the three-part form of the trilogy. Through the first-person narrative and the trilogy form Cary has achieved a multiplicity of views and shown the multiplicity of life itself.

CHAPTER VI

"THE FEARFUL JOY IS LOVE"

The Moonlight
A Fearful Joy

etween the trilogies, from 1944 to 1952, Joyce Cary published only two novels: *The Moonlight* and *A Fearful Joy*. Though related in general theme—they deal with women in love and the fearful joy of loving—these novels are entirely separate. However, during this period Cary attempted to write another trilogy which he never completed. This unpublished trilogy was to have the general title, *The Captive and the Free*, and the titles of the individual volumes were to be *The Captive and the Free*, *Easy Money*, and *Bow Down to Heaven*. It would be almost impossible and certainly unrewarding to examine the plots of this projected trilogy, for there exist manuscripts for three different versions and for two of these versions there are scenes written in both the first person and in the third person. However, the themes, characters, and techniques used in two of the versions are significant because they bear an important relationship to the two published trilogies and to the two novels of this period.

In these unpublished novels Cary experimented with the trilogy form. One of the versions of *The Captive and the Free* trilogy consists of three interrelated novels written in the first person and narrated by the three protagonists, each commenting on the lives of the other two; it is particularly significant because of its relationship to the form of the two published trilogies. This particular version is also significant because it bears a close resemblance to the central situation of the Nimmo trilogy. The central situation involves Major Gye, his wife Kate, and Lord Drummer, resembling the Nimmo-Nina-Latter triangle. Kate, because she is "passionately attached to son and wants place for him" allies herself with Lord Drummer; she has come to hate her husband "for his lack of control but is guilty too and good to him." She falls in love, but Major Gye in a fit of jealousy loses control, shoots at Lord Drummer, and is jailed.[1] However, Kate loses Lord Drummer to Doatie Pilcher, his secretary. Doatie, as Lord Drummer's wife, is the first person narrator of the second volume, *Easy Money*, rather than Kate, but her book, like *A Prisoner of Grace*, is a defense of Lord Drummer.

The resemblance of this version of the unpublished trilogy to the Chester Nimmo trilogy is even more remarkable on closer inspection. In a version of the beginning of *Easy Money* written by Cary in 1949, Doatie Pilcher says:

> I'm told its no good to bring libel actions against the papers on the way they have written lately over the Lord Drummer case, because Lord Drummer was convicted and there is still so much prejudice against him. So I am writing this book instead. And first of all, it is simply not true that Lord Drummer was a common swindler. He was most generous, kind hearted person and I have nothing against him. It is only fair that I should make this plain because Lord Drummer tried to shield me at the trial when the Crown council asked if I was not a gold digger who had married him. And when Lord Drummer answered that I had been chosen as his social secretary entirely because of my high character [council tried] to shew that I had had many expensive presents from him.[2]

There are basic differences between this and the Nimmo trilogy: Lord Drummer is not a politician but a speculator in lands and stocks (the "easy money"), and he is convicted in court of swindling; Doatie is not his former wife helping him with his memoirs, but his former secretary who is first his mistress and then his wife. The central situation involves the public morality of economic speculation rather than the public morality of political practices. Yet the similarities are significant and reveal how Cary made use of this material for *Prisoner of Grace*. Not only is *Easy Money* a defense of the reputation of Lord Drummer by his wife, and thus of her own reputation, as Nina's book is of Lord Nimmo and her own reputation, but a basic theme of the book—to get at the "truth" of events and human relationships—is the same.

A third-person version of *Easy Money* illustrates how closely its resemblance to *Prisoner of Grace* depends on the use of the first-person narration. Though the central situation involving the Lord Drummer case is unchanged, the objective third-person narration removes the element of personal defense in the above passage, and since the element of "truth seeking" is implicit in the role of the detached narrator, this theme is objectified by the impersonal point of view. The opening lines of this version illustrate the difference:

The little woman at the corner of the bar was drinking whiskey & talking about the Drummer case to two young men who stared at her as if in inquest and a middle aged woman, stout and rather smartly dressed in black, whose expression changed up and down. . . .
The talker was about forty but had a strangely yellow, wrinkled face, much older than her hair & figure; & yet preserved. It seemed like an artificial flesh. "Of course I'm a bit out of touch" she was saying "I came out this morning—out of gaol I mean. I didn't mean to tell you that—I don't care—I don't give a damn."
. . . "And you think poor old Drum was an awful scoundrel. He wasn't a scoundrel at all. He didn't mean any harm. He was father—yes father. He makes me laugh." She smiled lustily and then made a face as if she were going to cry.[3]

That Cary directly used *The Captive and the Free* material in the early stages of writing the second trilogy is evident in the following early version of *Prisoner of Grace:*

My Aunt Barfoot is a remarkable woman. Truly. She brought me up and I ought to know. But what is remarkable about her is not her career or her opinions, as most people think, or her politics which are nonsense, but something else which is quite different. She's *really* sensible—almost too much so. Its sometimes quite shocking, as now. For when I'd told her everything, she said only "I can see you're one of us." "What, Aunty," I said. "I mean you're a regular Latter, like me. You take what you want." "But Aunty, you don't think" "Now don't you pretend to be a fool" she said "You're not such a fool as that—you wanted that Guy man [Major Gye] and so you went to him. "Oh Aunty, do you think so," for I was quite shocked by this idea. "Now, don't be shocked at yourself" said Aunty "You're a Latter born, and that's just what a Latter would do. And what of it?" [4]

Nina (named Dinah in this version) is pregnant, and Aunt Latter suggests she marry Phil Maxin, a clerk in Aunt Barfoot's estate office. Dinah is surprised by the suggestion and protests at first, but she soon agrees. Aunt Latter comments:

"You've done a wise thing" said Aunt Barfoot to me "Phil has a future in front of him—he may be quite an important man. He is not too clever or well educated but just enough and he has the gift of the gab. Besides he believes all this radical nonsense about making a new world—as if you could make a new world without new people to put in it." [5]

Phil Maxin is an early version of Chester Nimmo, with all the essential elements: ambition, radical politics, oratory.

Major Gye, Jim Latter's prototype, is the narrator of *The Captive and the Free,* the first volume of this unpublished trilogy:

People say I'm a nice chap. That's my reputation. But its not really true. The truth is I'm an easy going chap who made up his mind, a long time ago, to enjoy life. Even as a child,

I remember, I could enjoy life about twice as much as other children, especially some of the lively ones. . . . I had a good steady appreciation of all good things from peppermint balls to fishing. . . . It remains also . . . as a quality of my whole life. For I still enjoy good things.[6]

The similarity between Major Gye and Captain James Latter is evident in the style itself: the directness of the soldier's mind and the simplicity of his narration. Here, as in *Not Honour More*, is the basic insistence on getting at the "truth" of things ("its not really true. The truth is . . ."). And while Major Gye as "an easy going chap" differs from Jim Latter's uneasy seriousness, both share a directness of behavior as well as of mind. In his jealousy and in the directness of his response to it (attempting to shoot Lord Drummer), Gye most obviously resembles the Jim Latter of *Not Honour More*, and like *Not Honour More* Gye's book is a defense of his action. Less obviously, but perhaps more importantly, both are conservative men with a soldier's sense of duty and honor, and both relate the corruption of private morality to the corruption of public morality.

Another passage from Major Gye's narration is even more directly related to *Not Honour More* and its love triangle:

I'd begun to have warnings abt [about] my wife. . . . I had evidence enough, on the legal line, to satisfy any jury. So I had to ask myself "Shall I shoot the fellow, or go to law and divorce Hannah." And the answer was that it would be a damn shame to win the girl & break old Henley's heart, just because Drummer was a dirty dog & took advantage. "Dammit" I said to myself "What are the real facts. Hannah is still a young woman & shes never been what you call in love with me. She don't [sic] love Drum either. In fact, she used to dislike him a good deal & the only reason why shes been especially nice to him was because he was so damned ugly & because Leila used to treat him like dirt. Hannah . . . has a soft heart and besides, she hates injustice. She cant bear to see people taken advantage of. She was always sorry for Drum and took trouble to be kind to him.[7]

This passage, however, is not included with *The Captive and the Free* manuscripts; it is an isolated holograph sheet found among the manuscript rejects of *A Fearful Joy*, and therefore does not represent an actual version of *Easy Money*. Though it anticipates *Not Honour More* with its characterization of Hannah who like Nina has a soft heart and hates injustice, as well as its central situation of the love triangle, it is also related to *The Moonlight* with its suggestion of the relationship between the two sisters, Hannah and Leila. Perhaps it represents an intermediate version of *The Captive and the Free* begun when Cary saw the possibility of exploring further the relationship of two sisters, for Hannah and Leila are the two sisters whose contrasting lives are the central focus of the second version of *The Captive and the Free* trilogy.

The second version of *The Captive and the Free* involves not only a different set of characters, but also an entirely different approach to the material.[8] Although it is not related to the second trilogy in theme and character, it is like the two novels of this period, particularly *A Fearful Joy*. This relationship is not as direct as the relationship of the first version to the Nimmo trilogy, but it is equally significant. It emphasizes the continuity of theme and characterization with *The Moonlight* and *A Fearful Joy*. Indeed, from the portrait of Sara Monday to the portrait of Nina Latter, Cary presents a series of studies of women in love, and this unpublished version of *The Captive and the Free* trilogy provides further insight into Cary's portrayal of a woman's world from a woman's point of view.

The successful portrait of Sara in the first trilogy led Cary into a further exploration of the world of women as the world of feeling. In a note on *The Captive and the Free* trilogy he writes:

Women create in the realm of feeling. (like Sara) they operate with and in feelings including their own Their reactions are not merely personal, they make personality and *read novels* because novels deal with personality, the vital stuff. They explore this realm in themselves and with others —sometimes consciously, sometimes blundering into all obstacles, blindly.[9]

The creativity of women in the realm of feeling is dramatized in Sara and Nina, Ella Venn and Tabitha Baskett, and Hannah and Leila Kentish, the two sisters of this version of *The Captive and the Free*. In a continuation of the above note Cary contrasts the two sisters in terms of their emotions: "Hannah does not blunder but she is reckless and hasty, contemptuous of danger and so she falls into holes. Leila is instinctive, the passionate and impulsive." [10] A further note on *The Captive and the Free* explicitly reveals Cary's intentions:

Captive and free. Applies to special position of women. Study of women's characters—in *different* generations.
Not only Hannah. But Leila, Cassie, Bertie, and Gina. . . .
As background 1. Change of *idea* of women's position. Shewn operating in women's minds. 2. General ideas. Battle of life and its necessities. Men in politics. R. Chamley Nigel.
Method. Women's minds and scenes—the men seen through them. But *not rigid*. Give mens remarks. in womens view.[11]

The phrase, "in *different* generations" is a clue to the similarity between this version of the unpublished trilogy and *The Moonlight* and *A Fearful Joy* (and thus its fundamental difference from the Nimmo trilogy), for it is a family chronicle. Like *The Moonlight* and *A Fearful Joy* the scheme for *The Captive and the Free* covers the late Victorian period through modern times when the younger generation takes over. A series of notes on *The Captive and the Free* reads like an extension of the notes on the projected volumes of the *Castle Corner* series:

Attachment to the *ideas of life*, which leads to tragedy because of the *changes of life*. . . .
Background, the injustice due to free creation. . . .
Captive of circumstances of *civilization* which gives *freedom*. Hannahs *battle with injustice*, with care, from which she can't escape. . . .

Period 1920–1940 of confusion gradually *taking a new form*
—a more oganized social form. . . .

People in a "period" are not typical of the "period" because
of their characters but because of the effect of the period
upon these characters formed usually in a previous period.[12]

This is not to suggest that Cary revived the *Castle Corner* scheme to write *The Captive and the Free*, *The
Moonlight*, and *A Fearful Joy;* but rather that one of the
most fundamental themes in Cary's writings, which goes
back to the African novels, is the tragedy caused by attachment to beliefs which have become outmoded and
the injustice caused by the free creation of ideas.

Probably this second version of *The Captive and the
Free* postdates *The Moonlight* and antedates *A Fearful
Joy;*[13] therefore, it is unlikely that Cary made use of this
version for *The Moonlight*, which has a more direct and
immediate source. The relevant similarity is that both
works have as their central focus the relationship between
two sisters, suggesting that Cary wanted to explore further the possibilities of this contrast and clash of personalities. The conflict between Leila and Hannah Kentish, like that between Ella and Rose Venn, is based in
differing personalities and emotional attitudes toward
life: "Leila wants intensity, magnificence, and urges
Robert etc. to aim high—take the big chance. Feels the
grandeur of religion as Hannah feels necessity and neatness and moral value." [14] Hannah is the rationalist "loving
order, *neatness*, and young things. Captive of sex in her
plainness . . . and *sense of obligation* to people." Leila,
in contrast, is the freer spirit, "artistically creative, likes
magnificence, richness, intensity, high church. Fights for
these. intriguing, not very truthful or scrupulous." [15]
Like Rose, Hannah is the captive of her sense of duty
but "understands her captivity and fights *for truth*, for
judgement." [16] Like Ella, Leila is "instinctive . . . passionate and impulsive." [17]

Despite its similarity to *The Captive and the Free*,
Castle Corner has a variety of characters and settings

and is diffuse in its effect; *The Captive and the Free* concentrates on a few characters, all the major ones being women. This concentration on a few major characters and on a woman's view of the world relates *The Captive and the Free* to the two novels of this period rather than to *Castle Corner*. Ella's daughter Amanda and Tabitha's granddaughter Nancy illustrate the rebellion of the younger generation in *The Moonlight* and *A Fearful Joy*. Leila's daughter Roberta rebels against the values of the older generation and finds herself "captive of the impalpable cage of her own egotism & lack of love and *duty* i.e. she has lost a *habit of the soul*." [18]

Although the use of the two sisters suggests a relationship of this version of *The Captive and the Free* to *The Moonlight*, its chronicle of events and ideas more closely resembles *A Fearful Joy*. The current of history flows through *A Fearful Joy*, sweeping Tabitha Baskett along with it. The projected plan for *The Captive and the Free* surveys the same revolutionary period of history as it affects the lives of the characters. But one essential difference, aside from the more leisurely pace afforded by the trilogy form, is that Cary's use of the historical present tense in *A Fearful Joy* creates a sense of immediacy and heightens the illusion of swift changes, whereas the use of the past tense in *The Captive and the Free* creates a slower, more reflective flow of events. [19] Yet all the novels of this period portray varying aspects of the same fearful joy—love.

THE MOONLIGHT (1946)

The Moonlight, Cary writes in the preface, "sprang" from two different sources: first, from his "violent reaction" to Tolstoy's *Kreutzer Sonata*; [20] and second, from the story of "an elder sister left in charge of a family, who brought them up at the cost of her own happiness (she refused her lover) and was rewarded by being feared and detested" (page 11). Some years before the story of the elder sister came to his attention, Cary began writing an answer to *The Kreutzer Sonata:*

It was to be the exact reverse of *The Kreutzer.* An old woman in a railway carriage (instead of Tolstoy's old man) was to tell how she had murdered her sister for preventing her daughter's marriage. And in the course of the story, she would give the true case for women as a sex, the real dilemma of a girl who is held by nature in so firm a grip . . . [page 10].

Five or six chapters of this first version of *The Moonlight* were written, but then it was laid aside "perhaps because of some interruption or counter attraction." Years later the story of the elder sister became the *donnée* for the published version of *The Moonlight,* and Cary remembered the old version, "but when I began to read it I felt at once . . . that it was no good to me. . . . So I tied it up again, and it is buried somewhere in the rattantoo which fills the darkest and dustiest corner of the attic" (page 11).

Unfortunately, I have not been able to find the manuscript of this first version of *The Moonlight,* but there is ample evidence in Cary's notes for the second version that he did not abandon his original purpose of writing a counter book to *The Kreutzer Sonata.* He writes: "Anti-Kreutzer. A FAMILY. *The quality of love and religion in women.*" Similarly: *"The lust motive.* Anti-Kreutzer. The world may die of sophistication of the *private happiness* of freedom—it may die of freedom. But then it will rise again because of passion, and poetry, all art, will arise out of the passion—and this is God's (or natures purpose)." [21] And the novel—with its symbolic title, its theme of love as a fearful joy of body and soul, its direct reference to Tolstoy's ideas refuted by Ella's feelings— is itself an answer to Tolstoy's *Kreutzer Sonata.*

The story of the elder sister Rose and her relationship with Ella dominates the narrative of *The Moonlight,* but

thematically it is used to reinforce the anti-Kreutzer
theme, thus unifying the two seemingly disparate and opposing views of love and duty. This is achieved by relating the conflict of ideas to the Victorian period. Cary
intended Rose to be a Victorian woman "of character
and unselfish goodness, who had sacrificed her own happiness to her duty," and he was surprised, though perhaps
he should not have been, "that critics and correspondents
almost all looked upon Rose as a 'typical Victorian tyrant'" (page 5). Rose has all the trappings of the Victorian tyrant—the strong will to dominate, the almost
religious devotion to duty and, as the corollary to that
duty, the compulsion to interfere in the lives of others
in order to preserve the sanctity of marriage and the
family. Yet Rose is as much a victim of that tyranny as
she is herself an example of it. When her mother dies
suddenly she, as the oldest daughter, understands her
duty to care for her father and take the place of her
mother, even though it means sacrificing any possibility
of marriage and personal happiness.[22]

Cary's notes on *The Moonlight* describe the Victorian
mores which he recreates in the novel: "The Victorian
family is its own lawgiver (thru father) and is jealous of
any intrusion from outside, legal or political. *Injustice
will be put right in heaven*."[23] Love of father and love
of family are the cornerstones of this law: "The law of
the family is the law of conscience, evangelical, superior
of [sic] man made law—The law of love, forbearance,
all to be put right in Heaven, as Rose believes." The religious life of duty and the real life duty of marriage
and family are one and the same: "Christian marriage as
family centre. The family as centre and *marriage as
centre of family*—that is the moonlight—devotion—the
fountain—the creators of family—priest and creator."
Authority is not seen as tyranny: "Authority in family
enforced by *love and conscience*."[24]

Ella comes to understand the nature of Rose's sacrifice
and devotion, but authority, whether tyrannical or pater-

nalistic, breeds rebellion: "Rose as high priest of Vict. Family. religion dominates and *necessarily provokes rebellion*." [25] Ella falls in love with the aesthete Geoffrey Tew, of whom Rose disapproves because she recognizes in his ideas a threat to her ordered world in which self-sacrifice has moral meaning. To Rose physical love is disgusting: "Rose has Victorian disgust—it has grown on her—*out of the sublimation*—it was the Victorian fault —the overbalancing of its romance." [26] Her sense of duty to family must be a higher, spiritual love, or else the sacrifice of her personal happiness is meaningless; but she "felt the danger of Tew's arguments . . . because her breast was open to them" (page 72), recognizing her vulnerability as a woman to passion. To Ella, her love for Tew is sacred: "I was in love with all my soul, and if my body was excited it was part of my soul. Yes, that's why I was not ashamed—why, it was so splendid, what incredible happiness" (page 93). This is Ella's triumph: it is at once a refutation of Rose's idea that sex is disgusting and a refutation of Tolstoy's idea that sex is the root of all evil.

Ella, however, lacks Rose's strength of will. She recognizes her weakness, and it is that, not her love for Geoffrey Tew and later for Ernest Carnage, which she regrets: "Oh, what is true—what can one believe—except this pain—this shame. . . . That I left him—oh, how could I be so weak?" (page 93). It is not a weakness of character, but a sense of guilt that she may be wrong and Rose right, for Ella, though a rebel in her feelings, is bound by her conscience to the Victorian ethic. She is a divided soul, caught between the truth of her passion and the morality of her age. She accepts the Victorian moral order because she knows no other and tries to reconcile it with her emotions; she "hates the vulgarisation" of sex she observes in the younger generation; she "hates emphasis on its *importance*, its *sacredness*, especially to women, if religiously conceived, i.e. if conceived as the crown of love, and the source of motherhood and a womans sacred function. This enrages her against Tolstoy—'That disgusting old man.' " [27] In contrast to the younger generation Ella, the Victorian rebel, seems old-fashioned, holding on desperately to the "truth" of outmoded ideas: "She is the old age disintegrating among the modern," Cary writes in another note, for her "own *essential tragedy* is that she can't get out of her period; and neither can Amanda." [28]

Amanda represents the emancipated modern woman of intellect. Born of a relationship that violated the Victorian sense of propriety as well as of morality—Ella's affair with Ernest Carnage, a married man—she represents the dissolution of the Victorian period. Yet she is as much a victim of her emancipation as Ella and Rose are victims of their enslavement to Victorian ideals. Her intellectualism is a denial of her womanhood which, Cary suggests, is unnatural. Though Amanda in some ways resembles D. H. Lawrence's Miriam of *Sons and Lovers* and Ursula of *The Rainbow*, Cary's theme is quite different from Lawrence's. Cary states the difference: "Theme is—*not* D. H. Las [sic] but the *religious life* of *duty* as a *real life* and one that is *founded on nature*." [29] Rose's religious life of duty is to her father and to her younger sisters as the "mother" of the family; it is a real life founded on the natural organization of the family and meaningful within the framework of the Victorian moral order. Ella's duty, though she constantly rebels against it, is also to the family; and though she accuses Rose of tyranny, she acquiesces in giving up Geoffrey Tew and in giving up Amanda because of her conscience and guilt, which is a recognition of her duty. Amanda's duty is to her own nature as a woman, which she denies, but which Ella tries desperately to awaken by matching Amanda with Harry Dawbarn.

Amanda, like her mother, is a divided soul: "She is quick and sensitive and feels with her mother—and what attracts her is the fundamental *sense of womanhood* which awakes and revolts against the intellectual life." [30] But her intellectualism is dominant; she cannot at first surrender herself to the earthy farmer Harry Dawbarn. While her mother plays the "Moonlight Sonata," she resists Harry's lovemaking: "I don't quite like being stirred up like that, it's rather humiliating. It's so mechanical. It makes one feel like one of Pavlov's dogs. Harry *scatters* one so frightfully. And I must get on with my work." [31] In a symbolic scene Amanda's rejection of her womanhood is linked with her rejection of Victorianism. The Victorian woman is seen not as a sacred saint beatified by Christian marriage and motherhood, but as breeder, "a sensual victim and machine, a fleshly device for the production and nourishment of other little lumps of flesh, a creature as little free or noble as the segment of a tape worm" (page 150). The imagery is modern, "scientific," antiromantic. The light of the moon in Amanda's room, which is filled with Victorian furniture, illuminates a past age, but moonlight is reflected light—no age can fully understand the immediate past against which it has rebelled. Ella must speak for the Victorian period, but even her illumination is reflected light, living only in her memory, and she cannot communicate with Amanda.

The moonlight is a complex symbol based on the romantic myth surrounding Beethoven's "Moonlight Sonata" but also stemming from the classical mythology of the moon as the symbol of love. To Amanda it is a symbol of her unemancipated body:

the sight of her own white and plump leg thrust into the moonlight startled her into a new horror—of herself. She felt her own flesh, and it, too, was part of this hideous world of the flesh. She, too, was a woman; meat for lust; a walking womb; a cow to yield milk; a slave to nature, which had given her a heart only that she might be a servant to her reproductive organs. An animal constructed from top to toe only to continue the species, so that life should not perish from the world [page 150].

In contrast Ella, whose favorite music is the "Moonlight Sonata," remembers how she had surrendered to the sensual music of Geoffrey Tew's poem:

See in the moon, moon-flesh
Caught in the shadowy mesh
Of dreaming lilies.
Oh girl, your beauty's whiter.
Noon of your breast yet brighter.
Your swoon more still is
Than rapture of all lilies [page 70].

When Amanda finally submits to Harry Dawbarn, it is a surrender to her nature without happiness or fulfillment: "It seemed to her . . . that this was bound to be her fate, and that she was strangely resigned to it. . . . 'I mustn't expect happiness, that's the mistake. No, I mustn't ask, am I going to be happy, or am I being happy? I must simply do what has to be done'" (page 216). Amanda becomes pregnant, repeating the pattern of her mother's past.

However, Amanda never marries Harry Dawbarn; all of Ella's efforts are ineffectual. Ironically, Amanda again repeats her mother's history by becoming involved with a married man, but with an essential difference—whereas Ella loved Ernest and expected to marry him, Amanda's relationship with Robin Sant is intellectual, passionless, and unromantic. In a parallel situation Robin, the modern man, is divided in his nature; he seeks intellectual companionship with Amanda, but achieves sexual satisfaction with his wife Kathy who, as a foil to Amanda, has "no ideas beyond having a house and a husband and a car and tea parties." [32] Amanda is instinctively attracted to Harry's earthiness, but is happiest discussing ideas with Robin. In the crucial scene in which Robin decides to divorce Kathy and marry Amanda, the imagery is symbolic. While Robin and Amanda *talk* about marriage, divorce, and sex, Harry and his partner old Bob mow the hay as the sun sets: "The dark red sun, as they began to climb the slope, illuminated only their heads, and the long bladed scythes which shone as if wet with thin blood, as if the fresh-cut grass had bled upon them" (page 168). The images of red and blood associated with

the sun and with Harry are in contrast to the previous
scene in which Amanda is revolted by the sight of her
flesh in the moonlight: "The moon was now passing
down behind the tops of the trees, and the shadows of
the leaves, on the short grass of the lawn, made a pattern
like Brussels lace against oyster-coloured velvet, on which
the beds of roses, seeming in the pallid light like artificial
copies of the real, stood motionless like embroideries." [33]
Amanda's mood is a cold, indifferent light in contrast to
the hot sun: "She let her dressing-gown fall back so that
the cold wind blew between her breasts, and looked
around her not at visions, but at trees, grass and sky. 'A
lot of space and some indifferent vegetables,' she said to
herself" (page 150). Nature—trees, grass, sky, and her
own womanhood—is not a romantic vision but empty
space and indifferent vegetables. At this point Robin appears at the window in the moonlight, "a white motionless
figure like some ghost peering out" (page 151).

Images of whiteness, coldness, and death recur in the
crucial hay-mowing scene. As darkness falls and the moon
is hidden behind a cloud, "the mowers appeared as silver
shapes on a grey field; steel men moving through an un-
substantial underworld" (page 170). As the darkness
deepens, an artificial moonlight is created when Harry
turns on the headlights of the Ford: the light "gave to
the bushes and the alley, the hollows of the ground, the
aspect of a moon-photograph, in black and white, and
made the house-wall spring out of the dark, like some ash
precipice of the same landscape" (page 172). The artificial moonlight (which is itself reflected light) distorts the
figures of the mowers so that they appear like "two
enormous scythemen" whose motions seem like a medie-
val dance of death. Robin himself explicitly states the
death theme though he intends it facetiously—"Father
Time and Brother Death" (page 173).

In a parody of romantic love Amanda and Robin go to
bed, passionless and sexless, for the sole purpose of giving Kathy evidence for a divorce; it is a travesty on

love, and the imagery is of death: "Amanda, *cold and stiff*, got into bed and stretched herself out, making herself *narrow*. In a minute Robin's *cold* body slipped down beside her" (page 173, italics supplied). The death motif becomes explicit as the mowers say good-night: "The old man slightly moved the scythe which stood beside him like a kind of banner, and raised his skull-like face with its great hollow eye-sockets" (page 174). And the next morning when Amanda awakens, just before Kathy enters the room, she looks at Robin who sleeps "so deeply and quietly that he seemed dead. His features had the smoothness of the dead . . ." (page 174).

Amanda never marries Robin, for though Kathy may lack Amanda's quality of mind, she knows what she wants and knows how to hold on to it. Like Bessie, Kathy has the toughness of character to preserve her marriage. Amanda immerses herself in her work, but it is no compensation for the loss of love: she waits in despair with a feeling "of pity and emptiness; not self-pity, but a universal pity as for all the loss, the frustration, the waste, in the world, and the emptiness was the shell of this pity. It lodged in a vacuum, without object, without will or hope or love. It was merely a vast still grief" (page 315). She is unfulfilled and waits for a miracle to happen. That it has happened, or at least could have happened, she fails to recognize. As she repeats her mother's history and waits for her baby to be born, she does not understand her mother's life—the miracle of love, the miracle of creating new life. Ella, victim of the Victorian social order, was denied happiness but achieved fulfillment; Amanda, victim of modern ideas, denies herself happiness and never achieves fulfillment. Even her work, the fruits of her emancipation, bores her at the end.

The futility of her life is her denial of nature; moonlight is reflected light, it needs the sun. In an unpublished note on the theme of *The Moonlight*, Cary writes: "The cool light of womens judgement is their yen,—it bathed the world—Men were a sunshine hot, dusty, unfaced in detail, deceitful, self-deceiving. But the moonlight was not its own source—women lived in the moonlight. Women by nature, cool, calculating—after the first passion. Suspicious, fearful." [34] Ella knew the source of moonlight though it made her feel guilty; Amanda thought she could live without the source though it was given to her. By their nature as women they live in the moonlight, but whereas Ella sought the sun, Amanda sought to be her own light. Amanda's tragedy is that she is the victim of her own freedom which substituted for the Victorian enslavement the injustice of suffering by one's own free choice.

Though the novel ends with Amanda, and a great deal of narrative action is concerned with Amanda's dilemma, the true narrative and thematic center of the novel is Ella. Professor Wright suggests that *The Moonlight* fails as a novel because it "has no sustained 'commanding centre': Ella who is meant to fulfill this role, is too often pushed aside. . . . When Ella dies the book itself dies." [35] But if Ella seems to be "pushed aside," it is an intentional device; and since her death does not take place until the penultimate scene in the last chapter of the novel, it can scarcely be said to harm the novel. The narrative of *The Moonlight* shifts rapidly back and forth in time, and the great achievement of the novel is the reconstruction of the past so that it becomes a living commentary on the present. As Robin and Amanda talk glibly about sex in the modern manner, calling it a dirty game, Ella dips into her memory for reassurance and affirmation: "I was in love with all my soul, and if my body was excited it was part of my soul. Yes . . . it was so splendid, what incredible happiness" (page 93).

Thus Ella is sometimes "pushed aside" because she is an anachronism to the younger generation, a relic of the Victorian past that has been discredited and displaced. Never a strong-willed or dominating personality in her own time, she is ineffectual as a manager of lives in the modern age; Amanda and Robin scarcely listen to her, and her nieces and nephews who do not listen to her at all are introduced to develop the theme of the gulf between the past and the present. Even when Cary necessarily shifts from Ella's viewpoint in order to develop a scene in the present—as with Amanda—Ella remains the central focus. The structural pattern of the narrative—the alternation of past and present—consists of both the alternation from within Ella's point of view (for example, her affirmation of love for Geoffrey Tew as a refutation of Robin's and Amanda's attitude) and from without Ella's point of view (for example, Amanda's denial of her flesh in the moonlight). But what lies outside Ella's viewpoint is nonetheless integrally related by the narrative structure of the novel and by its theme.

Ella's death and Amanda's final despair are contrapuntal scenes and form the thematic climax of the novel. Ella is convinced that she had murdered Rose, but this is taken by everyone else as evidence that Ella's mind is wandering. The "murder" is part of Cary's original, anti-Kreutzer version of *The Moonlight*, but he later substituted the intention of murder. Although Rose's death is accidental, Ella, Cary writes, "understands truth about death—that she willed it subconsciously—like a rebel." [36] She wanted Rose's money to help Amanda marry Harry, and when Rose changes her will to tie up the money, Ella "accidentally" loses the only copy. But Ella's attempts to manage lives are to no avail; Amanda will not have Harry, and even Harry becomes cautious. Ella's last desperate attempt to salvage the situation by selling the house (a symbol of the past) is doomed to failure. Indeed the only result of all her plans is that Amanda is left pregnant and unmarried. Although Amanda does not blame her for interfering, Ella takes upon herself the guilt, as she does the guilt of Rose's death: "Yes, I oughtn't to run away—I ought to admit the responsibility. Rose accepted her fate—such a hard and cruel fate" (page 307). She is determined to accept the responsibility of guilt as Rose accepted the responsibility of self-sacrifice. She will tell the police the "truth" about the "murder." She "accidentally" takes an overdose of sleeping pills and repeats Rose's death.

But life goes on, generation and regeneration; there is continuity as well as change, repetition as well as creation. As Ella gave birth to Amanda, so Amanda will give birth to her child. Amanda may intellectualize her life, but unheeding nature continues. She rejects the idea of abortion, suggested in desperation and guilt by Ella. As she accepts the child growing within her and thus accepts the continuity of life

the moon which had been recognized only by a pale blue illumination behind the cloud became a little brighter, so that the tree was not so sharply defined. But the great stretch of landscape behind, woods, fields, the Longwater . . . the hills and a triangle of the Atlantic seen between the cliffs. . . . All in fact was still background, only more complex and mysterious, to the minute distinction of the silver tree [page 306].

Though she feels now only a "vast still grief," she may come to know and feel the fearful joy of love: "At last Amanda lifted her hands and put them on her waist. She was growing big. She said to herself, 'But do miracles happen? It will be interesting to see'" (page 315).

A FEARFUL JOY (1949)

"This book," Cary writes in the prefatory essay to *A Fearful Joy*, "began a long time ago in the sketch of a young girl at her first dance, who gets no partners and is in despair, when suddenly she is taken out by the beau of the evening. He flirts with her, charms her, and finally elopes with her under the delusion that she is an heiress." [37] The basic elements of this plot are found in several unpublished stories, particularly in a short novel entitled *Facts of Life* and in the old beginning of *A Fear-*

ful Joy published posthumously as the short story, "The Ball." [38] *Facts of Life* combines the idea of the girl at the dance and the subject of the spellbinder which, Cary reveals in the preface, interested him at the time: "I saw that the two notions would go together. My spellbinder was to be the crook of the dance who, though a crook, set the girl free and gave her richness of life" (page 5). *Facts of Life* explicitly emphasizes the attraction the crook's reputation has for the girl:

The star of the evening was Toner who had just escaped prison by the skin of his teeth at the big smuggling trial of that year.

The arrival of Toner was the sensation of the evening, one of those successes that rewarded Mrs. Pratt for endless intriguing and a thousand snubs. . . .

Toner has been described as a crook. In fact he belonged to that vast world of half-crookery which includes everything from the woman who smuggles a bottle of scent to outside brokers selling doubtful shares at high prices. In this world Toner was somewhere about the middle. He was not a thief; but he did not enquire too closely into the origin of some of the cars that he dealt in. . . . He was not a confidence trickster, but he had taken thousands of pounds from fools on such scheme [sic] as a school for racing drivers. . . . As a smuggler, of course, he had certainly broken the law in a big way. But smuggling for some reason is not regarded as criminal, only as illegal. . . .

But the immense attraction of a man like Toner for a girl like Betty Wendt was his independence. As she saw him now walking across the room towards her he seemed like a creature from another world. . . .

[For] here was a man who had made his own world, who was in command of his own destiny, who was afraid of nothing and nobody. In fact Toner had for Betty all that charm described as mysterious of the crook for the adolescent, and the young girl barely out of adolescence and not yet out of its confusion, frustration and resentment. [39]

The original beginning of *A Fearful Joy*, "The Ball," "turned on the character of the girl, her humiliation at this first dance, her debut, so important in her life and in her idea of life; her gratitude to the man who distinguished her, and her loyalty to him afterwards" (page 5). In *Facts of Life* Betty Wendt is a pretty girl and, therefore, the emphasis is on infatuation rather than on rejection by other partners at her first dance. In "The Ball," as in the novel, the girl is unattractive, timid, and ungraceful, her only solace being her piano practice. She does not want to go to the dance, but her brother Harry, who has already bought the ticket, is determined that she make her debut, and her sister-in-law Edith has already bought her frock. She has no partner, but Harry escorts her to the dance and then leaves her. No one offers to dance with her, and she sits out the dances in a panic of loneliness and humiliation, until Bonser notices her: "one very handsome fair young man, the accepted beau of the party . . . suddenly raises his eyebrows at her so high that she smiles and her own eyebrows rise in sympathy." [40] Bonser introduces himself, claiming they have met, although he does not remember her name. He asks her to dance:

He conducts her with a firm grasp towards the ballroom. Tabitha seeing that he is sacrificing himself, would like to perform some extraordinary feat of devotion to shew her sense of his goodness. At the same time, she's still resenting his impudence. She is saying "But he didn't know me at all— he just wanted to introduce himself." [41]

Tabitha, in spite of her doubts, is grateful and flattered by his compliments: "She thinks 'But is it possible, can he mean it. Does he really see something in me. Is this how it begins?'" But when Harry takes her home after the dance he warns her against Bonser and says that she will never see him again because he's leaving town the following week. Tabitha is in despair; she sees herself returning to a life in which even her piano practice seems "painfully flat." When Bonser does reappear in her life, she is eager to accept a romantic view of him: "She says to herself 'But I believe he really is in love. It does happen like that.' " [42] She agrees to marry him secretly, and eventually she elopes with him.

Cary discarded this beginning; "the last thing I did when I had finished the book was to take out the first chapter containing the story. I saw that the book needed a solider, more historical first chapter." [43] Though he discarded "The Ball," he used much of it in the first part of *A Fearful Joy*—the basic elements of the plot, the characters, and the narrative technique. As in *A Fearful Joy* the Bonser of the original story has pursued Tabitha because he believes she has a fortune; similarly, Bonser postpones marriage, using the excuse that there is some difficulty over his birth certificate. They live together in a hotel, Bonser bets their remaining money on the races and loses, and they skip the hotel bill. The original manuscript ends with Tabitha deciding to face it out at the hotel because she does not want to face a life of moving from one hotel to another without paying; but Bonser leaves.[44] Thus, the fundamental aspects of Tabitha's and Bonser's characters and the basic elements of their relationship are the same in the original beginning as in the published novel.

Another similarity, the use of the present tense, raises a problem of technique. What is suitable for the short story in which the intent is to show Tabitha swept into a relationship with the carefree Bonser is not suitable for the novel in which the intent is "to lay bare historical change not just as a surface, but in its roots" (page 6). Cary achieves his picture of the "whole world seeking escape from boredom, from insignificance, in everlasting invention and experiment" (page 6)—but he does not expose its roots.[45]

Indeed, toward the end of the novel the swift-moving historical events of the late 1930's and the war itself are so glossed over that the effect is of a fictionalized outline of history in which the characters are cardboard illustrations of typical Englishmen and Englishwomen reacting to newspaper headlines. Only the surface of events is given, and only the immediate reactions of the characters are recorded. The lack of a central reflecting consciousness merely emphasizes the superficial approach to the historical changes. Cary cut to the bone many passages between Tabitha and Nancy, her granddaughter, which might have given balance to the historical part, but already the novel was quite long, and he felt that the theme "of the permanent characters that underlie all change (of rebirth and renewal)" (page 7) did not need further development. Cary himself reveals doubts about this approach:

I am told that the book is too packed, too fast moving, but I meant it to move quickly to give the sense of that driving change, of that world revolution which is so sharply present to our feelings even from hour to hour. But the critics may be right. Since change is relative, I might have got my sense of movement less in succession of events than in contrast with some large permanent character . . . [page 7].

Cary's working notes on *A Fearful Joy*, as well as the preface which was written three years later, state again and again the broad theme: "Whole theme of backgnd is change, emergency—due to inventiveness." The "theme & feeling of book is *urgency of inventive change*, of youth & *creative drive from life itself*." [46] The theme of creative renewal is the background against which the lives of the characters are the central focus; the characters gain added significance from the background of events and are not used, as in *Castle Corner*, merely to illustrate the general theme of change. Cary recognized this fundamental approach to the composition of the novel in his notes: "Fearful joy personal to Tabitha, not in background which shews ordinary battle of *ideas, passions*, to *use life*." [47]

The fearful joy is Tabitha's love for Bonser, and it remains at the core of her life throughout the novel, through all the reversals and changes. But as the novel develops, as Tabitha's experience of life enlarges, the fearful joy takes on a larger meaning: "Fearful joy applies at end to *whole experience*—not *only* to Bonser." By this method of expanding the specific meaning of a fearful joy, Cary relates the foreground to the background theme: "The fearful joy is that of life itself—living always in the new experience and its natural morality is that of the adventurer, the explorer, the creator (in imagination) the lover who ignores convention." [48]

Tabitha Baskett begins as a rebel, running off with Bonser against her family's wishes, and ends up a conservative, questioning the new represented by her granddaughter Nancy; yet paradoxically, her rebellion is a quest for orthodoxy in marriage and in her duty as a wife and mother, and her conservatism is an affirmation of the creative renewal of life through change. "In a world so profoundly creative," Cary writes, "what is not in creation withers away; and nothing . . . can stay alive to the experience unless it be continually reborn and re-created to the imagination" (page 8). Yet "in our experience of change, we are also aware of the permanent. We could not have the one experience without the other" (page 6).

Bonser's function in the strict narrative sense is to provide the catalyst which moves the story along. More importantly, his reappearances are used to set Tabitha free and give her richness of life "again and again, as at each stage of her life she ran aground in some grievance, some despair" (page 5). The lifelong struggle between Tabitha and Bonser is in the larger sense the struggle between permanence and change. Tabitha seeks stability in their relationship, but Bonser, like life itself, will not stand still; even when he is dying, he rebels and tries to escape from Tabitha. Yet, underneath the surface of their struggle is the permanence of their love, however changing; it is the permanence of renewal, like the permanence of the recurring seasons.

Bonser is a carefree man existing on the surface of life

like Mister Johnson and pursuing a dream of riches. Against the background of changing ideas and events his roguery seems shallow and opportunistic, but it is this very background that gives meaning to his superficiality. In contrast to the dedicated and committed lives of the rival *Bankside* editors, Dewpark and Manklow, who become bitter enemies in the war of ideas and live embittered lives, defending ideas which are rejected by the younger generation, Bonser is happy and carefree and lives an imaginative life of his own. In contrast to Gollan's dedication to his business and his sense of duty during the war, Bonser's life seems useless and wasted, but it is Bonser not Gollan who gives Tabitha happiness and the fearful joy of love. And though Bonser may seem at times to be only on the periphery of events, he becomes at crucial times the center of Tabitha's life and sets her free from despair and loneliness. When he dies, Tabitha articulates the worthwhileness of this seemingly worthless man:

"But where would I be if he had not come: an embittered old woman these last twenty-three years, a miserable useless old woman, and probably dead long ago. He brought me to life again; it was like a resurrection from the dead. . . ."

For Bonser, that danger and burden, has also been the ground and sky of her life. The loss of him seems to her, therefore, what the loss of a cover is to a book. What has appeared like a mere external addition, an expensive and heavy ornament, is suddenly perceived to be not only the chief support and protection of the whole, but the form of its existence . . . [page 359].

Tabitha, however, is throughout the novel in the middle of life. Unlike Ella Venn in *The Moonlight* or Cleeve Corner in *Castle Corner*, she does not exist on the periphery of the aesthetic movement: she is part of the movement. But, ironically, Tabitha, once so *avant garde*, becomes old-fashioned in contrast to her daughter-in-law Kit. She is directly involved in the war through her husband Gollan with his armament factories and his political connections, but her values and the values of her generation are rejected by the postwar generation represented by her granddaughter Nancy. All through these eventful years of rapid change she is too busy *being* to reflect on what *has been;* and the use of the present tense, while it intensifies the pace and underlines the theme of change, does not allow for the reflection which would analyze the events she experiences. To find meaning and permanence in the current of her life she clings to notions of family and duty which are rejected by Kit and later by Nancy. She clings to ideas, but ideas change and make her old-fashioned. She clings to relationships, but her son John dies in his youth; Bonser is forever escaping and finally dies; her husband dies; Kit resents her "interference" with Nancy; and Nancy leaves her to live a new life. Only at the end does Tabitha, herself dying, find that faith that gives meaning to her life.

The continuity of life itself is the final meaning of *A Fearful Joy,* as it is of *The Moonlight.* Tabitha in the beginning gives up religion, illustrating the rebellion of the youth of her generation, but in the end she returns to a personal religion: "Tab throws away religion as dogma & finds it again in *life, as wisdom.*" [49] Specific dogmas and moralities may change, and Cary suggests they must change as the condition of freedom, but the form remains permanent as the basis for values. Nancy, the "good-time girl of the twenties, as soon as she has her first child begins to create about herself those elements of order and responsibility that—in Tabitha's gloomy view—had disappeared from the world with the Victorians" (pages 6-7). Through Nancy and her child is seen the recurrent pattern of Tabitha's life and its values of order and responsibility, love and loyalty, just as Nancy's postwar rejection of Tabitha's generation is the recurrent pattern of rebellion by the younger generation against the old. This is the paradox of change: unless the old changes it cannot be reborn in the new; unless it is reborn it "dies." Whether it be a religion, a national idea, or a human relationship, it can live only if it is "continually reborn and re-created to the imagination."

The permanent forms of human happiness—love, family, imagination, and life itself—underlie the crowded surface of change. Cary links the paradox of change to the recurrence of the seasons and the renewal of life each spring to Tabitha's symbolic death:

> And some mysterious warmth rises in Tabitha to meet the warmth of the sun. It is like a sap, which diffuses through her nerves a sensitivity, so that they respond not only to the sun, warmth, but to all the life about in its complex of feeling; to the middle-aged leaves, still strong under sentence of death; the parched grass; the flowers in the beds, watered that morning, but already running to seed and soon for the rubbish heap; the children in their absorbed animal existence, their passionate ambitions and fears, their brutal angers . . . [page 387].

Her rebirth is an affirmation of life. She is seized with laughter, the laughter of life itself, the fearful joy, at the moment of death. She prays to be reborn:

> And the prayer that is torn from her is not to the father or the son or the spirit. It is the primitive cry of the living soul to the master of life, the creator, the eternal. "Oh, God," her blue lips murmur, "not quite now" [page 388].

She is reborn, and as "she looks again at the sky, the trees, the noisy quarreling children, at a world remade, she gives a long deep sigh of gratitude, of happiness" (page 388). Life is renewed and the fearful joy of life is reaffirmed. "Unless the world *is for happiness* (in achievement)," Cary writes, "*it* is nothing, *stupid*." [50] Tabitha finds her life meaningful and happy, despite all the terrors that it can hold, and her life is a microcosm of the world itself.

CHAPTER VII

"POLITICS IS THE ART OF HUMAN RELATIONS" THE SECOND TRILOGY

Prisoner of Grace
Except the Lord
Not Honour More

*T*he second trilogy more closely resembles the triptych scheme than the first trilogy for which Cary had originally devised the analogy. The essential difference, however, lies not in technique, which is basically the same, but in treatment of character. Whereas Sara Monday is unsophisticated and unable to comment on art and history, Nina Latter is both sophisticated and reflective, and thus able to comment on the history of the times reflected in the lives of her two men, Chester Nimmo and Jim Latter. Cary was conscious of the need to make Nina an intelligent and reflective narrating consciousness. In a note on *Prisoner of Grace* he writes: "Nina is not another Sara. Sophisticated, dreamy, understanding all round. . . . She is sympathetic, *reasonable*, pagan, rather French. . . . Intense pleasure in contemplation and reading. *Intensely happy* & knows it." [1] Thus *Prisoner of Grace* is not as self-centered as *Herself Surprised*, and indeed Nina's avowed purpose in "writing this book" is to defend Chester Nimmo and herself against "revelations" attacking their characters. As a result, the focus of the second trilogy is on Chester Nimmo.

127

This emphasis on Nimmo is a modification of Cary's original concept of the trilogy as a three-fold multiple view of three characters, as in the first trilogy. In *Except the Lord*, Nimmo's own memoir, there is little of Nina and nothing of Jim Latter, so that the effect of the trilogy is to create a character-center, Chester Nimmo. It is true that in *Prisoner of Grace* Nina does reveal something of Jim Latter's personality as well as Nimmo's, but it is Nimmo who dominates because Nina is his prisoner of grace; and it is true that in *Not Honour More* Jim Latter presents another view of Nina as well as of Nimmo, but of the two it is Nimmo who dominates. *Except the Lord*, like its parallel in the first trilogy, *To Be a Pilgrim*, is mainly a revelation of the past in which the other two personalities of the trilogy had no part. As in *To Be a Pilgrim*, with its emphasis on the Protestant tradition "which is the soul of British and American democracy," [2] in *Except the Lord* Cary "tried to get at the roots of left-wing English politics in evangelical religion." [3]

"Reality," Cary writes in "The Way a Novel Gets Written," "is one whole. Religion is full of aesthetic feeling and political action; politics uses aesthetic and religious appeal; every man is born into a society which is at once constant in its primitive natural elements, the natural family relationships, the need, passions, and ambitions of all human nature; and highly flexible in its larger groupings of tribal, national, and moral obligations." Cary's idea of reality explains why he uses fundamental human relationships, particularly the changes from generation to generation within a family, to reflect "a political idea, a nation, a world idea," [4] as he does most explicitly in the family chronicles, *Castle Corner* and *A Fearful Joy*. It would be misleading to suggest that the private lives of the three protagonists of the second trilogy are an allegory of English democracy and that the marriage of Chester Nimmo to Nina Latter is the marriage of Protestant democracy to capitalism,[5] but it is fruitful to suggest that their private lives present a microcosm of the world at large:

> *Prisoner. Background* the universal political position—the necessary management of human nature and human beings all different and all trying to make their own lives in their own way—not always selfishly but always individually so that you have domestic politics in every nursery and politics so called is not a unique case but simply the public form of a universal case.[6]

Cary did not want to write a novel about government and politics *per se*, but about a human being who in his public life is a politician. "Politics is the art of human relations, an aspect of all life," Cary writes in the preface to *Prisoner of Grace*. "That is why I wanted to tell the story through the eyes of a wife whose marriage needs a great deal of management. I wanted to give the complete political scene." [7]

Nina's role as narrator is a complex one, for the truth is complex. The occasion for her narrative is stated in the opening sentence of the novel: "I am writing this book because I understand that 'revelations' are soon to appear about the great man who was once my husband, attacking his character, and my own" (page 9). Her function as narrator is not merely to defend Chester Nimmo and herself against these "revelations"; it is to tell the "truth" about Nimmo and herself. Thus Nina's "book" must be more than Sara's, a frank revelation of the past as in a "memoir" or "confession"; it must also present a perspective on the past both personal and historical. Nina must be, as Cary writes of her in his preface, "essentially a woman who can understand another's point of view" (page 8). To achieve this perspective he used the device of enclosing Nina's qualified judgments in brackets: the brackets "make Nina a credible witness. They enabled her, even in the first person, to reveal her own quality of mind. She had, in short, a brackety mind" (page 8).

Nimmo's character, both public and private, is essential to the trilogy, and Nina must be a credible witness to his career. But she can be credible only if she understands herself as well as others; Cary achieves this by having Nina look back on herself as though she were viewing another person:

Chester central. the whole thing must be cast in the form of memory where Nina looks at herself as at a stranger (or an actor on the scene—her interest in the small) and comments on her youth and assumptions. So she can watch her own development as well as the mens. And can *describe* scenes atmospheres and their *effect*.[8]

"It is not true," Nina declares at the outset of *Prisoner of Grace*, "that I was trapped into marriage, when I loved someone else. If there was any deceit, it was on my side" (page 9). The "truth" of Nina's denial of being trapped into marrying Nimmo lies not in the "fact" of her pregnancy, but in the self of "the creature that I was then." The "I" that drifted with events and the "I" that passively accepted marriage with Nimmo, the "I" that loved Jim Latter and the "I" that came to love Chester Nimmo, the "I" that compromised itself for the sake of Nimmo's career and the "I" that is a prisoner of grace —"all these different I's" are the truth. It is a "fact" that Nina, pregnant for the second time by Jim Latter, was determined to divorce Nimmo and marry Latter but, prisoner of grace, she "discovered how wrong I had been to think that nothing could be changed in the 'real' situation because it rested on 'too solid facts'" (page 112). It is Jim Latter who, in his madness, insists on "facts" and "proofs"; it is Nina who, in her state of grace, knows that "the truth is quite different from the facts and much more complicated" (page 99).

The whole truth about Nimmo cannot be told by Nina because she does not know it. *Except the Lord,* Nimmo's own story, fills the gap left by Nina's account concerning his early life. As the record of the pilgrimage of a lost soul it parallels Wilcher's in *To Be a Pilgrim. Except the Lord* reveals the origin of Nimmo's political artistry in his father's evangelical oratory and the origin of his radicalism in the nonconformist temperament and poverty of his family. Politics and religion are linked together, just as in the first trilogy art was related to religion. Nimmo rediscovers his faith and in rediscovering it finds purpose in his life.

Though *Not Honour More* is necessary to complete the portrait of Chester Nimmo, of all the novels of the two trilogies it is least able to stand by itself. It is the last book of the trilogy, and Cary could hope to depend on his readers having read the other two novels. He uses Jim Latter's point of view in *Not Honour More* to show "the clash between two fundamental temperaments . . . that will never agree on the ends or even the means of political action." [9] Thus the main purpose of *Not Honour More* is to present a balance in the trilogy between the two opposing political views of Nimmo and Latter, the democratic compromiser and persuader as against the uncompromising and dictatorial man of direct action. Cary connected this conflict of public politics with the conflict in the private lives of the three protagonists because he saw their private lives as a microcosm of the political macrocosm.

Cary gains much more than he loses by presenting the point of view of Jim Latter. By remaining true to Latter's character he paints a convincing dark portrait of Nimmo, but it is the very excess of Latter's fanaticism that defeats his (Latter's) evangelical mission to destroy Nimmo as a public symbol of democracy and as a private image of love. If one were only to read *Not Honour More*, one would be equally convinced of Nimmo's evilness and of Latter's madness; but if one were only to read *Except the Lord* and *Prisoner of Grace*, one would, ironically, never be wholly convinced that Nimmo was not a scoundrel both as a husband and as a politician.

Cary recreates the past through the first-person nar-

rative, the trilogy form, and the portrayal of personalities whose lives are the past. This past is unglossed by
veneration and yet through it runs the thread of England's protestant and democratic heritage. Chester
Nimmo—for all his intoxication with power, his public
and private compromises and immoralities, his ration-
alizations and inconsistencies in politics and in marriage—is motivated by an evangelical conscience to war
against social and economic injustices. The past of *Prisoner of Grace* is uncolored by sentimentalism, and yet
what emerges from the individual's defiant battle with
social laws and customs is the democratic ideal of personal freedom and public responsibility. Like Gulley
Jimson, Chester Nimmo is free because he is a man of
imagination, the artist of human relationships; but unlike Gulley, Nimmo's freedom is limited by public
responsibility.

The ultimate degradation of Nimmo as a political orator is seen in *Prisoner of Grace* when his "son" Tom (the
illegitimate son of Nina and Jim Latter) mimics his
"father's" mannerisms and speech in a night-club act.
In *Except the Lord* Cary reveals Nimmo's fascination
with his father's oratory which spellbinds the congregation; thus is born Nimmo the politician, the demagogue,
the spellbinder of his "congregation" in the days before
television. In *Not Honour More* Jim Latter sees Nimmo
as a power-hungry demagogue without honor, a corrupt
politician without principles. Yet these are only partial
views of Nimmo. Though he deliberately chose the art
of oratory to further his political ambitions, his early
radicalism has the fervor of righteousness at a time when
the liberal idea of social justice needs a spokesman to
give direction to the workers in their protest. Though
he married Nina knowing she was pregnant (by Jim Latter) in order to further his political ambitions, he is fond
of her and needs her, and it is she who defends his public
and private life against his enemies, Jim Latter in particular, and who forgives him his weaknesses. Though

in his old age, under the guise of needing her to help him with his memoirs, he sexually assaults Nina, now married to Jim Latter, Nimmo was more sinned against than sinner. He had forgiven Jim Latter long ago for being his wife's lover and had given his name to the children he knew were not his own. Although he compromised his political principles in the reality of practical politics and his moral principles in the reality of his marriage, he remains a man of principle. The portrait of Nimmo is a composite picture drawn from different perspectives in the three novels of the trilogy. The form of the trilogy with its multiplicity of views reveals the whole reality of Chester Nimmo.

PRISONER OF GRACE (1952)

Prisoner of Grace, and the idea for the whole trilogy, began with a note jotted down in a notebook.[10] Cary further reveals that he wrote first the crucial scene at the railroad station in which Nina becomes a prisoner of grace (page 7). The technical difficulties of writing this scene in the first person from Nina's point of view led him to try "the false first": "I gave Aunt Latter a brother, a retired civil servant devoted to Nina, and made him tell the story." This narrator, Cary continues, "ran away with the book and ruined it, everything was falsified and cheapened, the acuteness of the observer only emphasized his lack of real understanding, as sharp arrows will go right through a target and leave no mark" (page 8). The beginning of this version is as follows:

Our local great man is Nimmo, you can't imagine how much we think and talk about him, this may surprise you. Retired politicians . . . do not usually excite much interest, but Nimmo is one of those men who is bound to be talked about. He excites feeling; people either worship or loathe him, some do both.[11]

Like the rejected beginning for *The Horse's Mouth*, the objectivity and detachment of the narrator creates a remoteness from the central character which, as in Conrad's *Lord Jim*, is successful if analytical detachment and objectivity is the intention, but which, as in Cary's first trilogy, is self-defeating if the multiple point of view and the interaction between the trilogy form and the central characters as narrators is the intention.

This remoteness of the narrator as central observer rather than central character is best illustrated by comparing a passage written from the point of view of Aunt Latter's brother and a similar passage written from Nina's own point of view. First, the brother tells of Nina's pregnancy:

> And when Nina's disaster [her pregnancy] came (I can tell you all about that too if I think fit and find the right place for it) and Jimmy had bolted off to London, and Nina was walking about with a practically green countenance, and a look as though she had just been waked from a particularly bad dream and did not feel quite sure if it had stopped, Aunt Latter thought at once of Chester, in fact you might say that she jumped at the idea.[12]

Nina's version retains the immediacy of felt experience:

> And when the disaster came to me (if, as I say, looking back on it, you can call it a disaster) and Jim (having for once, poor boy, lost his head with me), and we were both completely at a loss what to do next, she [Aunt Latter] said to me one morning, "You're looking very green, miss. What's wrong with you?"
>
> "I don't know exactly, Aunt," I said, trembling all over.
>
> "And what's wrong with Jimmy; Why has he rushed off like this in the middle of his leave? I shouldn't even dream what I suspect if you weren't such a dawdling idiot."[13]

Nina's parenthetical remarks are not awkward afterthoughts, a storyteller's hasty reminder to himself to take up a point later; they are careful asides which reveal an attitude and make the reader want to know more about her and Jim Latter; they do not, as the uncle's aside, make the reader indifferent to the "disaster." Nina as narrator is the "true" point of view, for she *is* the prisoner of grace; her uncle as narrator is the "false" point of view, for he is the prisoner of the narrative.

The marriage of Chester Nimmo and Nina is at its outset a compromise and an expediency: he needs her money and her social position; she needs a husband for her unborn child; and each is aware of the other's need. It is no ideal love affair, and yet on the whole it is a successful relationship; and if it is not a marriage of passion, neither is it a marriage without love. The compromises and expediencies, the changes and shifts of emotions, the complications of divided loyalties reflect (but are not allegorical representations of) the larger world of politics.

Politics is the art of human relations, and Nimmo is the artist of politics practicing his art on Nina. He is a man of imagination, and for his own survival he has created a private world to the extent that he convinces himself that Tom is his own son; and yet this world is no less real than his father's evangelism which survives the failure of his prophecy of the Second Coming and the end of the world. Nimmo's political success, founded on the artificiality of oratorical methods, survives the compromises and expediencies of practical politics; but it is for these compromises and expediencies that he is attacked and condemned. "Chester has and practices imagination in all his relations," Cary says of him. "This is deliberate. He practices love in the same way. . . . He gives freedom to get her [Nina] back again. He allows her to go wrong in order that she may feel her load of guilt towards him and be more amenable. He needs her desperately, and simply can't bear the idea of losing her." [14] The discrepancy between the ideal and the real, between ends and means, whether it be in public affairs or in private relationships, is the area of human conflict.

Like Tom Wilcher, Chester Nimmo is no saint. As Cary comments, he is not "a completely admirable char-

acter. . . . He is an egotist like most successful politicians" (page 6). He is "on the make—very *energetic*
at pushing—but unconsciously so. i.e. gets on commit-
tees for good ends." [15] But the egotism and the ambitious aggressiveness has also its element of loneliness and
self-doubt. Chester is

The study of a character full of imagination in a world
run by imagination who often bewilders himself who therefore clings to stable elements in fear of utter loss of himself,
who is afraid of his own trickyness in inventing and argument
so he clings to principle. . . . So study through Chester of
world in the power of imagination and confused by it and
longing for some guide ruler religion etc. . . .

Nina must realize that he does suffer he is really in love and
that he darent risk losing faith in himself.[16]

Nimmo accommodates himself to the times, but he
tries to hold to his principles in politics, and he tries to
hold onto Nina and the children in the politics of his
personal life. Jim Latter is unable to accommodate himself to changing ideas; his attitude toward Nimmo and
politics is uncompromising. Without the art of compromise, Latter's way leads to dictatorship or anarchy.
Without the element of grace, his sense of honor is
empty and false.

As a prisoner of grace, Nina forgives Nimmo his sins
and weaknesses, both public and private, for not to forgive them is to condemn one's self. She sums up his
career at its crisis when he compromises his pacifist principles to join the war cabinet: "Perhaps Chester did
'get away' with lies and tricks and did help to 'destroy our
great cause.' But all leaders (who really drive and steer),
especially reform leaders, do destruction to a cause. Because they set out to make new worlds and new worlds
can never be so good (or so new) as people expect"
(page 263). Nimmo, like his father before him, foresaw
the end of the world, his world; but Nimmo as a politician sought to change it, patch it up, and make it do.
Ironically, he helps destroy his own world. Because he

had joined the war cabinet, he is later pelted with rotten vegetables by his constituents who blame him for the war and its aftermath; he is defeated at the polls; he admits that he has no children of his own; and he divorces Nina, losing her to Jim Latter. But Nina returns to help him with his memoirs and to save herself from "damnation."

The original title for this first novel of the trilogy was *Prisoners of Grace*. Nina of course is *the* prisoner of grace, but "The second prisoner of grace is her eldest son Tom, who is unable to escape from Nimmo's powerful influence, and whose life is ruined by his inability to get free and make a place of his own in the world." [17] Tom's mimicry is a parody of the politician as artist-orator, but it works both ways. While it mocks the tricks of the political spellbinder, it binds the mocker to an imitation so that he cannot get free and make a place of his own in the world. "What ruins Tom is his conscience. He must act Chester his masterpiece. And yet hates it and tries not to admit that it is Chester." [18] Chester used these oratorical tricks to get things done; Tom imitates them for the sake of an art. He represents "the free irresponsible world of art." [19]

It is characteristic of Cary's approach to the creative personality that his "artists" are romantic egoists whose behavior is at odds with society and more often than not outside the law. Mister Johnson and Charley Brown are criminals. Sara Monday, the "female artist," is put in jail for theft. Gulley Jimson, the supreme egoist, is in and out of jail. And Preedy, the "artist of the soul," in *The Captive and the Free* is threatened with lawsuits throughout the novel. Chester Nimmo is no exception, for although he is not a criminal, his actions, both personal and public, are interpreted as such by the voters; at the end of his career he is tainted by scandals and "revelations" which are accepted as the truth. He is vulnerable, but his is the vulnerability of the free man, the creative spirit. Cary chose to portray men of imagination as (at their best) eccentric geniuses (and at their worst, grotesque), not because of any predilection for eccentricity or because he wanted to make his task of gaining the reader's sympathy more difficult, but because he conceived of the imagination as an irrational power for good and evil and because he thought of freedom as a creative force for good and evil, destroying the old and creating the new. Gulley Jimson is a study of the limits of freedom in the creative imagination, the creation of creation itself; Tom Nimmo is the perversion of that freedom for mean ends. Jim Latter is the perversion of politics which leads ultimately to dictatorship. Chester Nimmo is a study of the compromise between freedom and responsibility, means and ends, principles and practice in the management of human affairs.

Prisoner of Grace is a detailed portrait of a man who both in his public and in his private affairs is vulnerable as a human being. Nimmo compromises his early radicalism by publicly denying his private belief in nationalization of the land: was this denial made only to win the election? It must be remembered that the Liberal Party's program did not call for nationalization. His marriage had reached a crisis at the height of the campaign: did Nimmo merely maneuver Nina into staying with him in order to win the election and to save his political career after he won the election? It must be remembered that although Nimmo "manipulates" Nina, using all his artistry, it is Nina who as prisoner of grace forgives him and stays with him. Nimmo, who had gained fame with an antiwar (Boer War) speech, and who had pledged himself never to join a war cabinet, accepted the position of minister of production during World War I: did he compromise his pacifist principles merely to remain in power? He did compromise his principles, and he was tempted by the offer of a key post in which he would have a "free hand," but he saw it as his duty and responsibility to the country to accept. "The P.M. says the country needs me—that I am indispensable. As Bootham says, it may be my duty—a moral duty—to change my mind and face the consequences . . ." (page 267).

Despite all his compromises in politics and marriage, Chester Nimmo is, as Nina views him, a good man "trying to do the right thing." Thus *Prisoner of Grace* attempts "to develop in Nimmo's political career, and his gradual education in the actual political world, the full theme of the political dilemma; that is, the old problem of means and ends." [20] What is needed to complete this study of Nimmo's political career is Nimmo's story of its nonconformist radical beginnings and Jim Latter's account in *Not Honour More* of its end.

EXCEPT THE LORD (1953)

The basic interrelationships of the three protagonists of the second trilogy are already worked out in *Prisoner of Grace*. In *Herself Surprised*, the parallel of *Prisoner of Grace* in the first trilogy, Sara makes a fresh start with each new relationship, but Nina is perpetually caught between two men and pulled in both directions. The lives of Nina, Chester, and Jim are so closely intertwined that Nina's story is necessarily the story of all three; and because Nina, unlike Sara, is articulate and "can understand another's point of view" she reveals the essential conflict and meaning of their lives. Therefore, Cary was free to explore different relationships in *Except the Lord*, rather than cover the *Prisoner of Grace* material from Nimmo's point of view.

The new subject is the origin and roots of Nimmo's political radicalism in the poverty of his family and in the nonconformist religion of his father. The new relationships are those within Nimmo's family—his father, his brother Richard, and most important his sister Georgina—and later those outside the family, particularly with the political radicals Pring and the Dollings.

Except the Lord takes up that period during which Nimmo is writing his memoirs with the help of Nina. We see Nina as a prisoner of grace from Nimmo's point of view: she "sits before me, pen in hand, eager to render me that last service of interpretation, anxious, as she says, to dispel through these memoirs a cloud of misunderstanding which has thrown so black a shade upon my last hours." [21] Though most of the novel is concerned with Nimmo's life before he meets Nina, the past, as in *To Be a Pilgrim*, gives meaning to the present. Nimmo's memoirs are not an "official" autobiography of a public man written with a view toward revealing his part in the political affairs of the nation (this has already been done by Nina). Instead, Nimmo says at the beginning, this is "the story of a crime, of a soul, my own, plucked back from the very edge of frustration and despair" (page 5). *Except the Lord* shares with *To Be a Pilgrim* the theme of a lost soul saved from damnation by the love of a woman: Tom Wilcher is saved by Sara's love, as he was earlier by his sister Lucy's love; Chester Nimmo is saved by Nina's love, as he was earlier by his sister Georgina's love.

The thematic structure of *Except the Lord* is circular; the novel begins and ends with Nimmo having visited Georgina's grave forty years after her death. He recalls that when he was a young man her dying words had renewed his lost faith in life and the Lord:

She was consoling me and it broke my heart—I felt then an indescribable shock of anguish and of exultation. And instantly among the turmoil of my senses a darkness fell away, great presences were revealed, things absolutely known and never again to be obscured, grief that I knew for love, love that I knew for life, joy that I knew for the joy of the Lord [page 286].

This conversion, an essentially Protestant renewal of faith through the heart rather than a rational decision of the mind, is revealed in the penultimate chapter of the novel. The final chapter is the reconversion of Nimmo "at the other end" of his life through the memory of Georgina's love: " 'Here,' I said, 'the story began and here it shall begin again' " (page 287).

Nimmo, as we know from *Prisoner of Grace*, is at the end of his career, a broken and defeated man, hated by his political enemies and even by those who were once his most ardent supporters, and reviled by the public who, as Nina says, believe "the worst of a famous man." In *Except the Lord* Nimmo is in despair because of these attacks:

Now again, at the other end of my life, an old and broken man, I am thrown into the gutter, I sit and wait for the night, the last darkness.

I am told that my whole career has been a disaster and a fraud. That great party . . . to which I gave forty years of my life, in which I rose to honour, lies in ruins, and those who lately filled the streets to cheer me on my way, long only that I should die. I am an embarrassment to them [page 274].

In this black mood he goes to stand at Georgina's grave. His conversion at the end through the spirit of Georgina that lives in his memory is also his final salvation through the grace of Nina: "she who has been my wife, my nobler soul, the close and secret comrade of my darkest hours, who has given to me more than her youth, her life and loyalty" has given "the perpetual knowledge of a truth that is truth's very substance, the faith of the heart" (page 214). The two women, the two conversions, the past and the present, merge; and, similarly, the two beginnings, his early political career and his return to politics late in life (as described in *Not Honour More*) unite and complete the circle. The "crime," his loss of faith both early and late in life, is expiated as he returns to his father's faith, and his soul is "plucked back from the very edge of frustration and despair." Nimmo, now near the end of his life, has "grasped the full significance of that profoundest of truths not only for the man but for all his endeavours . . . that unless he aim at the life of the soul then all his achievement will be a gaol or a madhouse, self-hatred, corruption and despair" (page 284).

The style of *Except the Lord*, so different from *Prisoner of Grace* with its air of wordly sophistication and secular affairs and from *Not Honour More* with its air of frenetic self-justification and perverted sense of honor, is reminiscent of *To Be a Pilgrim*, for both share the same basic religious theme, the salvation of a lost soul, and the same evocation of the past through the memory of an old man. "Style biblical," noted Cary. "I say to you—the repetition as in psalms the rhetoric and quotations. The descriptions of nature as the house of the greater god—the immeasurable power—the eternal soul." [22]

The biblical style permeates the whole novel because religion permeates the lives of the characters. Nimmo's father, a Baptist preacher, taught his children the fear of hell: everyday life is a high drama of good and evil in which the wicked are punished and the good are rewarded. "Far from doing us children harm," Nimmo asserts, "it was a sure foundation to the world of our confidence. . . . For we saw its justice, we knew, in the common phrase, exactly where we were . . ." (page 9). But the adult world is not so easily divided between the good and the wicked.

The play Chester Nimmo attends at the Lilmouth Great Fair is the central scene of the first part of the novel. It is a religious crisis that, in Cary's words, "puts him in conflict with [his] father." [23] To the son of a Baptist minister the play is a forbidden sinful pleasure in which "men and women practised feigning as an art, to deceive and confuse honest souls" (page 87). But his older and more sophisticated brother Richard told him the story of the play was really true. As Chester enters the "temple of lies" he says to himself, "But this story is true. There is no sin in a true story truly represented." [24]

The melodrama—the wicked landowner forces himself

on the virtuous cottager's daughter by threatening to raise her father's rent and evict him if necessary—is to Chester a morality play acting out the fundamental truth that the good shall be rewarded and the wicked punished. Thus God is not mocked; good triumphs over evil in the end. The play has its political overtones: "I knew also," Chester says, "the power of the landlord to oppress, and the weakness of poverty in self-defence" (page 92). The identification of the poor with good and the rich with evil is to Chester a true representation of life; it becomes the source of his militant radicalism.

But the most significant impression the play makes on the young Chester is the artistry of the actor in arousing the emotions of his audience. "But I also understood a power that I had seen exercised by my father also—though in a lesser degree—the spell of the orator" (page 99). Thus is born Chester Nimmo the politician, the spellbinding orator. The showmanship, the tricks of emotional oratory, the mannerisms and the gestures—all of which Tom mimics in *Prisoner of Grace*—are a revelation to Chester of a mysterious power. The actor's tricks are the basis for Nimmo's future success as a political orator, but his family's poverty and his father's evangelical fervor are the real basis for his sincere indignation at social injustices.

The climax of the first half of the novel is Chester's crisis of faith when his father fails to predict the Second Advent. The failure of the prediction does not lessen the father's faith, but it results in a crisis of faith for the children. After his loss of faith, politics becomes a new religion for Chester. The second half of the novel deals with his career as a political agitator, culminating in his active part in the Lilmouth dock strike and his disillusionment with political action.

Thus is born Chester Nimmo the radical political agitator. Under the direction of Dr. Dolling, the Tarbiton representative of the Proudhon Society, Chester becomes committed to radical political theory. But Dolling is a theorist; it is through Pring and Pittway that he becomes involved in political action, culminating in his activity in the Lilmouth strike. However, Chester Nimmo as a political agitator remains an uncompromising idealist; he resigns from the strike committee in a disagreement over policy which would compromise his principles. His loss of faith in Pring and Pittway is a revulsion against the violence and hatred unleashed by the strike and more fundamentally against the abuse of power they represent. Disillusioned and again without faith, he returns home to Georgina and Richard and to his father and his father's religion. Then his sister's dying words cause a rebirth of faith.

It is with this conversion that Cary ended the novel in the manuscript version sent to the publisher and set into galley and page proofs by the printer. After Cary corrected the page proofs, however, he added the final chapter, Chapter 62 of the published version. In addition, the first four chapters of the novel were also revised after he received the page proofs. Although Cary revised his proofs heavily, the addition of this final chapter is not typical of his practice.[25] The galley proofs of *Not Honour More* are extensively revised for stylistic reasons, but the changes in the page proofs of *Except the Lord* are textually significant.

Cary wrote his publisher concerning the revisions:

The form of the book is good and the proof are better than usual but I am much dissatisfied with my own work, especially at the beginning, so I am doing a good deal of rewriting in the first chapter. It will make *all the difference* believe me to the book. . . .

I earnestly assure you that this work on the first chapter transforms the book. Walter Allen was obviously worried about me and I saw what he meant as soon as I saw the proof.[26]

In a holograph postscript he added: "The *beginning* of a book is ¾ of the battle."

His "battle" with *Except the Lord* began long before
the revision of the page proofs. The original manuscript
version of the opening paragraph reads as follows:

I am an old man and they want me to die. I should be less
of an embarrassment to them. You have read in the daily
Press the speeches of the young telling me, in the crude but
powerful word of this latter day, where I get off. They say
that my policy, and that of the government which I served
so long, was one of blindness and deceit, I am told that I
cheated the people with words while I stole away their substance, that I shut the window on the day-light of truth and
opened the gate to the wolves.[27]

Cary rewrote this beginning paragraph of Chapter 1,
and the following version appears in the first page proofs:

Yesterday I stood by the grave of a noble woman—one of
the three noblest souls that I have ever known, my mother,
my sister and my wife. It is repugnant to any man to draw
back from the sanctuary of family life that curtain which
protects its innocence—I do so only in honour to the dead,
and in the conviction that the story I have to tell is pertinent
to that fearful crisis which shakes our whole civilisation from
roots to leaf, from sap to fruit.[28]

This revision is a change in substance; the original version emphasizes the political aspect of Nimmo's life, but
the revision emphasizes the personal and family life and
subordinates the political, which is more consistent with
the focus of the novel. Other than stylistic changes which
Cary made in page proof, this version is substantially the
same as the published text. However, the initial revision
of this paragraph did not make clear the chronological
connection between *Prisoner of Grace* and *Except the
Lord*. By the insertion of the phrase "an old man nearing
my end," Cary corrected the confusion by showing that
Except the Lord begins at about the point where *Prisoner
of Grace* leaves off.

Cary substantially revised the page proofs of the first

chapter, particularly the material on Nimmo's father. In the published text this material is sifted largely through the selective memory of the narrator, presenting a specific dramatic incident at the end to illustrate Mr. Nimmo's difficulties as the religious leader of the community. In the original version this material contains a considerable amount of narrative summary of the father's past:

Those were bad times for farmers, and a series of cold and wet seasons had ruined many richer men than my poor father. But I think there was another reason for his failure—he was a dreaming man who could not give his mind to buying and selling.

He had married late and, as they say, above himself, the daughter of a schoolmaster, and was himself a man of rich though uncoordinated learning, and wide experience. He had been a soldier and a miner before taking up the farm at High Fallow.

But the reason of his absent-mindedness was not so much his memories, or even the doubtful state of our fortunes, as his religious studies. He had been brought up an evangelical, first among Wesleyians, then as a Baptist, and for many years now he had been a lay preacher with his own small flock.[29]

In Cary's revisions the summary of antecedent narrative material is kept to a minimum. It is revealing to compare the concrete dramatic incident described at the end of the first chapter of the published text with the generalized passage which ends the first chapter before its revision:

I recall with great vividness another scene. My father is going to market—five of our black-faced sheep are penned between two gates and I am flattered to think that I am guarding them while my father harnesses the mare.

Suddenly a huge red man appears from the hill—he speaks to my father, argues, begins to wave his great fists. . . .

Now he is shouting and his words appal me, "How about your Jesus then?" and then, "You set up for a Christian and let a man go to Hell for ten shillings."

My father, a small figure, thin, already grey-haired, answers sharply, "If I gave you money, you'd only drink it. And what are you doing here?" [page 6].

. . . .

[. . . so that while he was at market and should have been concerned with prices of sheep or cattle, how they were moving and what were their prospects, he was too often preoccupied with the profounder motions of some poor cowman's soul, or the terrors of death as they appeared to some farmer guilty of thoughts, and perhaps of crimes, that he dared confess to no one else.][30]

Throughout the first four chapters, and also in Chapter 43, Cary revised both content and style. None of the correspondence with his publisher directly mentions his addition of the final chapter, which is the most substantial change Cary made in the novel, as a novel. However, Mrs. Winifred Davin, literary advisor to the estate of Joyce Cary, suggested to me that Cary probably had in mind this additional chapter when he sent the manuscript to the publisher but waited to see how the novel shaped up in proof. There is no doubt that the final chapter adds considerably to the meaning of the novel and rounds out its thematic structure.

The artistic achievement of the final chapter is to bring the novel full circle to its beginning with Nimmo standing at Georgina's grave: "here the story began and here it shall begin again." "Nimmo's second conversion, at the end of his life, is a new beginning, for with renewed faith in the Lord he will make another start in politics. In a larger sense, however, Nimmo's new beginning is death itself, for death—Georgina's and his own, soon to come—is a beginning to a man who has rediscovered his soul. His beginning "in the things I lived with" will be repeated in the young cruelty of the world, for his story, as he says at the beginning and at the end, is the making of a soul, which each new generation and each new individual must discover and rediscover for himself as the conditon of freedom. Nimmo, like Tom Wilcher, speaks for himself and his generation.

NOT HONOUR MORE (1955)

Prisoner of Grace ends with Nina trapped in the insoluble dilemma of her devotion to Nimmo's career and her love for Jim Latter. As Nimmo's prisoner of grace she "dare not turn Chester out" of her husband's house; he needs her help, and she would be "committing a mean crime against something bigger than love" to abandon him when he has suffered a heart attack and is at the edge of despair. She is the victim of her own forgiveness and grace; she is held to him by "a thousand ties that I should never break," and to refuse to help him would make her guilty of destroying his chance for a comeback in politics at a time when she believes the country needs his leadership. She knows that Nimmo's presence is a grave threat to her marriage and happiness with Jim Latter. She knows that Nimmo's sexual assaults are a real threat to her life because of Jim's suspicions already aroused by gossip, his hatred of Nimmo, and his soldier's sense of honor. She uses all her "political" skill to prevent a showdown, but the implication is that it is only a matter of time before the crisis ends in violence. Yet she prefers death to damnation: "I am terrified of 'damnation,' for it would destroy my happiness and all the joy of my life, and Jim can only shoot me dead" (page 402).

Prisoner of Grace ends with these words. *Not Honour More* begins, "This is my statement, so help me God, as I hope to be hung." [31] We know that the crisis has ended violently. The three novels of this second trilogy are closely related chronologically: only a month or two separates the end of *Prisoner of Grace* and the events described in *Not Honour More*. Thus the trilogy scarcely moves forward in time from the first to the last novel.

Cary's approach to history in the second trilogy is the opposite of the family chronicle method used in the *Castle Corner* series and the reverse of the historical present used in *A Fearful Joy*. The events of history from the 1860's to the 1920's are evoked through the memory and point of view of characters who have made history. The present is made to stand still while the past is unfolded, but the past is a reflection of the present. Thus this approach achieves depth of characterization and complexity of theme.

It is evident from his notebooks and worksheets that Cary, while still working on the first two novels, kept in mind the basic interrelationships of the three major characters as he wished to resolve them in *Not Honour More*. Some of the notes on *Not Honour More* date back to the first two novels. In a note on *Not Honour More* dated July, 1953, just before the publication of *Except the Lord*, Cary writes about the two opposing views of Nina:

> Jim says that Nina no conscience no honour. Chester says the most conscientious person he knows. . . . She has this power of happiness of content she forgives herself everything but unkindness and she is afraid of vengeance of the Lord.

> The two are close together about Nina and it excites them both. . . . Nina is like a primitive force of nature. . . . Chester understands this and gives the truth and also reverences the God in Nina.[32]

The crux of these two diametrically opposed points of view is the difference in the essential character of the two protagonists: Chester, though he accommodates and compromises his principles in the practical "politics" of family and nation, is capable of conversion and thus understands the power of grace; Jim, though he is "honest" and uncompromising, is incapable of grace and thus incapable of understanding and forgiving Nina. This paradox of the lost soul, saved by grace to give the truth, and the "honest" man, damned by his sense of honor to present the false, is pinpointed by Cary in another note, dated September, 1952:

> Jim's point of view. she [Nina] is a flirt and infinitely false. . . . She deceives Nimmo often with Jim and wrecks

Jims life. the "disaster" is her fault. because of her cold passion. . . .
Note all this suggests simply a study of the false. but the book is *study of Jim* as honest man among the crooks and time servers.[33]

Jim's "honesty" is a limitation of his own character which makes him incapable of understanding the weaknesses of others and certainly his own; not having fallen, he cannot rise to a state of grace; not having sinned (as he really believes), he cannot understand the human condition; not having lied, he cannot tell the truth. Partial views of reality are also the result of limitations of character, for "too solid facts" are deceptive clues to "reality." Like Mr. Ramsay's "facts" in Virginia Woolf's *To the Lighthouse*, Jim Latter's facts are uncompromising, but as with Mr. Ramsay the elements of compassion and self-understanding are lacking in him.

Not Honour More, of all the six novels of the two trilogies, is least able to stand on its own as a novel, and if it is read first it is a perplexing and unsatisfying experience for the reader. However, this is not the result of artistic weakness or failure, but of the form of the trilogy itself and of the essential character of the narrator. What is revealed in *Not Honour More* is not a third complex personality—indeed, Latter's personality is so simple and direct it needs little analysis—but an alternative view of Nimmo as a politician, a view which "shows the clash between two fundamental temperaments" in politics. Thus, whereas *The Horse's Mouth* is the recapitulation and climax of the first trilogy, *Not Honour More* is the reversal and anticlimax of the second trilogy. The two trilogies are essentially different, therefore, in their final effect, the first trilogy resembling the three-part classical sonata form in its development, and the second trilogy more nearly resembling the triptych folding back on itself, which Cary originally planned for the first trilogy.

As Professor Wright points out, "the reader must be

certain that Jim Latter is not Joyce Cary's mouthpiece, but that he is a fanatical man standing condemned on his own testimony." [34] It is a tribute to Cary that Jim Latter's story is presented so convincingly that the illusion of his honesty is complete. Yet, *Not Honour More* is the confession of a murderer, and its point of view must be considered in the light of self-justification. Jim Latter is scrupulously honest about the facts he presents, but his facts are selected, almost unconsciously selected, to justify his sense of honor and honesty. His rigid soldier's sense of honor is uncompromising, and it leads him to the attempted murder of Nimmo and the actual murder of Nina.

It is "true" that Chester Nimmo "compromised" Nina by embracing her, but Nimmo has forgiven both Nina and Latter much more—adultery. What is lacking in Jim Latter's code of honor, and what is essentially lacking in his character, is the element of forgiveness; he does not forgive Nimmo as Nimmo forgave him. Of course, from Latter's point of view, Nimmo's act of forgiveness was a selfish move to avoid a scandal which would ruin his career. Yet the reader knows from *Prisoner of Grace* and *Except the Lord* that the motivations of Nina and Chester are complex and that the truth of their relationship is deceptive. Nina, though she really loves Jim, believes in Chester as a good man and is held to him by her sense of guilt and her capacity for grace. Chester, because he loves and needs her and because he understands her, uses every artful trick first to hold her and then to win her back from Jim; without her grace he is lost. Both are "dishonest" in their behavior, but paradoxically it is Jim Latter's "honesty" which is the greater evil, for unable to understand and forgive the actions of others, he is unable to understand and forgive himself.

Jim Latter's lack of sensitivity is consistent with his character, but it makes *Not Honour More* a novel singularly lacking in complexity of theme, characterization, and style. From this viewpoint, *Not Honour More* is a weaker novel than the other two, or as one reviewer states it, "a lesser Cary." [35] But the same writing rule—"character first"—which led Cary to cut out Sara's notions of history and art in *Herself Surprised* applies also to Jim Latter as the narrator of *Not Honour More*. The insensitive terse style is wholly consistent with the narrow soldier's mind of James Vandeleur Latter, "late Captain 21st Hussars and District Officer Nigerian Political Service, retired." Cary immersed himself in the violent and vehement ego of Jim Latter, and the style arises out of the character of the narrator, not the character out of the style. Therefore, *Not Honour More* should be compared not with the complexity of *To Be a Pilgrim*, *The Horse's Mouth*, or *Prisoner of Grace*, but with the simplicity and directness of *Herself Surprised*.

The three-part structure of *Not Honour More* corresponds to the three major crises in the novel. The first part involves the personal crisis of the three protagonists in their entangled relations: the opening incident occurs when Jim Latter, returning home earlier than expected, accidentally happens to see Nimmo "interfering with my wife"; he shoots Nimmo but only wounds him. Latter's motivation at the moment is personal, to defend the honor of his home, but the larger and deeper motivation is political. To Jim Latter, Chester Nimmo is an evil man who has "destroyed all truth and honour in the country," as he has destroyed "the sanctity of the home and marriage." The personal and political motivations are intertwined, but it is the personal element that dominates: it is basically this concept of honor that Latter is defending. He will not make public a statement to the press unless Nimmo's assault is given as the reason for the shooting (he shrewdly recognizes that without it Nimmo would be made a political martyr), but the newspapers refuse to print the "truth," for the truth is libelous. "It's only your word against him," a reporter tells him. [36]

Yet, what is the truth? Cary explores in this novel, as he has in others, the relativity of truth, the partial view of reality, that occurs in the area of human conflict. It is true that a scandal would ruin Nimmo's political comeback and that he suppresses the truth to avoid the scandal. But Nimmo realizes a scandal would destroy his efforts to solve the national crisis brought about by the general strike; Latter's way leads to anarchy or dictatorship. Nimmo in the past has forgiven Jim Latter far more than this present attack, although it is true it has been to his political advantage to forgive, and he is motivated by a genuine desire to protect Nina. It is true Nina is implicated in the scandal, but she is motivated by the belief that Nimmo is a great man and that the country needs his leadership and not by unfaithfulness to Jim Latter whom she really loves. Even Jim Latter comes to doubt the "truth" of what he saw, for he realizes that Nina may have pushed Nimmo away because she saw Jim's reflection in the mirror, rather than because she was resisting his embraces.

The second part of the novel centers around the public crisis of the general strike. Jim Latter, though reluctant at first, is given the command of the special guards by the watch committee headed by Nimmo. In this part the historical events dominate the private lives of the protagonists, but the personal conflicts continue in the background. Jim Latter is convinced that Nimmo wants him to have charge of the specials in order to immobolize him on the personal level: "I couldn't go shooting him while I was under his command. And I couldn't put out statements to the Press while I was a policeman" (page 121). While it is true that Jim is effectively silenced, it is also true that Nimmo recognized his ability as a soldier and commander.

The violence and the political maneuvering of the general strike focuses on the central incident of this part of the novel: the arrest of the Communist strike leader Pincomb by Special Constable John Maufe. In the act of arresting Pincomb, Maufe uses force, striking him on the head and fracturing his skull. Maufe is arrested for using unnecessary and unprovoked violence on Pincomb. Latter resigns from the specials because Nimmo's committee refuses to back Maufe. The trial and its aftermath form the central focus of the third and final part of *Not Honour More*.

The political and personal elements reach a climax in this final section of *Not Honour More*. Political maneuvering by Nimmo determines the outcome of the trial: evidence is suppressed; the truth is distorted; justice is not achieved. Jim Latter is right about what the truth is, but wrong about the absoluteness of truth and justice. Injustice and untruth exist as necessary evils of man's condition of freedom. *Not Honour More* is a further exploration of this basic theme of Cary's, and the trial of John Maufe is a further illustration. The injustice that ensues is not the result of an evil will, Nimmo's, as Jim Latter insists, but is the consequence of political compromises made by Nimmo as he understood his position, which was to prevent violence. The innocent, John Maufe and his family, suffer the utmost misery. The suppression of the truth by Nina is not an evil conspiracy with Nimmo, as Jim Latter comes to believe, but is motivated by an honest belief in Nimmo's judgment. Her own sense of guilt at having lied leads her to attempt suicide, and in the end she pays with her life at the hands of Jim Latter. The injustice suffered by John Maufe is not erased by the injustice done to Nina and Nimmo; Latter's crusade for honor and truth merely multiplies the fundamental injustice of the world.

The trial ends—Maufe is found guilty and sentenced to prison—at the moment Jim Latter discovers the "truth" of Nimmo's part in it. The political and personal crises reach a climax simultaneously as Jim Latter reads Nimmo's private letters to Nina about the Maufe-Pincomb affair, implicating both Nimmo and Nina in the manipulations that led to Maufe's arrest and conviction. Latter's first impulse and intention is to kill Nimmo, but Nimmo locks himself in the lavatory and dies of a heart attack, indirectly killed by Latter. Latter then turns to Nina: "I had to ask myself if I was capable of this great duty laid on me by a cruel fate" (page 304).

The final chapter begins: "I say I never loved this sweet gentle woman so much as now when I knew she had to die" (page 305). Latter's concept of honor, a soldier's concept of service to his country, leads him to sacrifice his love to his idea of duty as expressed in Richard Lovelace's poem: "I could not love thee (Deare) so much, / Lov'd I not Honour more." Nina must die "Because of the rottenness. Because of the corruption. Because all loyalty was a laugh and there was no more trust. Because marriage was turned into a skin game. . . . Because of the word made dirt by hypocrites and cowards. Because there was no truth or justice anywhere any more" (page 305).

Ironically, the newspapers report the killing as a sex murder; the "truth" is relative, and Latter's "honor" is an empty word. The scandal which Latter hoped to use at the beginning to destroy Nimmo is used to destroy Latter's sacrifice of Nina to his idea of honor. But Jim Latter is incapable of forgiveness; when Nina asks him to forgive her, he is only capable of saying that she must forgive him. As Cary states in an unpublished note, "Jim's honour. Point out only artificial. Highest honour to sacrifice oneself. Afraid of public opinion—of what people will say. This 'honour' is artificial, trivial, it is *really cowardice*." [37] There is more honor in forgiveness, sacrificing one's own sense of self-righteousness in recognition of common weaknesses, which Nina and Chester understand, but of which Jim is incapable.

Not Honour More completes the trilogy by completing the portraits of Chester Nimmo and Nina Latter. Their portraits have complexity and depth because we see them from three angles of reality. Jim Latter's self-portrait remains two-dimensional because his mind is two-dimensional, seeing reality in black and white, in bold outlines of right and wrong, good and evil, uncolored by complexity of motivation and unrealized by subtlety of line. Though *Not Honour More* seems to be a weaker novel because of the narrator's lack of self-under-standing, paradoxically it strengthens the trilogy. This final novel completes the main theme of the trilogy—that politics is the art of human relations. By showing the lack of it in Jim Latter, *Not Honour More* reinforces the idea presented in *Prisoner of Grace* and *Except the Lord*, that the element of grace and forgiveness is essential to the art of human relations.

CHAPTER VIII

"THE FREE *PERCEIVE* THEIR CAPTIVITY"

The Captive and the Free

*A*lthough Joyce Cary's last novel, the posthumous *The Captive and the Free* (1959), is skilfully edited by Mrs. Winifred Davin, literary advisor to the estate of Joyce Cary, it is an unfinished novel. There are obvious gaps in the narrative at two points, for which Mrs. Davin as editor has supplied the necessary facts, and as Lord David Cecil points out in the introduction, "some strands in the story, the marriage of Joanna and Hooper for instance, surely need further development; and the end of the book is a little indeterminate and confused." [1] Indeed there are notes indicating that Cary would have developed further the relationship between Joanna and Hooper, and all indications are that Cary intended to continue the development of the last chapter, for the final manuscript breaks off in the middle of a sentence a few paragraphs beyond the published ending. [2] Probably, as Mrs. Davin suggests in her editorial note, Cary would have "strengthened the bond between the beginning and the end—for this novel begins where it ends" (page 10); perhaps even adding another chapter to bring the novel full circle, as he did with *Except the Lord*. Beyond these apparent points of revision are the intangible improvements in style, the development of theme and characterization which Cary would undoubtedly have made; such improvements are evident in the manuscript revisions of every novel he wrote.

The Captive and the Free completes Cary's study of
the relationship between the artist and freedom. Gulley
Jimson and Chester Nimmo are free men because they
are creative artists and because they understand the inevitable condition of freedom, injustice. The very title of
this last novel completes the meaning of this theme:

> Captivity and freedom applies only to the mind. Everyone
> is engaged by his responsibilities, he is captive to some kind
> of duty, but he may still be free in his general grasp of the
> whole situation and his attitude towards that situation. He
> can accept the world as he knows it has to be. He can under-
> stand that any good he gets out of it is a gift. That love and
> beauty which makes [sic] life worth living are inseparable
> from the evil of its contingency. He must *know* God, he must
> live *in* God.
> The real captivity, that is, is in superstition, hatred, fear,
> egotism, jealousy, in all the blind passions good and bad which
> bind men even when they realise that they are being bound
> and driven. . . .³

Gulley Jimson is the captive of his art, but paradoxically it is the creation of beauty which makes him free.
Chester Nimmo is the captive of politics with its compromises and practical decisions, but it is Nimmo's "grasp
of the whole situation" and his skill as an artist of human
relations which free him from the captivity of blind passions that bind and drive men like Jim Latter. In *The
Captive and the Free* the faith healer Walter Preedy is
the captive of his spellbinding powers, but it is his religious intuition which sets his soul free.

Cary had portrayed religious zealots before, Elizabeth
Aladai and the Reverend Coker in *The African Witch*
and Nimmo's father in *Except the Lord*, but they are not
the central characters and their significance is not the
central theme in these novels. From his first novel to his
last Cary was concerned with fundamental questions of
faith. In his preface to *Aissa Saved* he writes: "Ethics are
important enough, goodness knows, but the fundamental
question for everybody is what they live by; what is their

faith." [4] Such novels as *To Be a Pilgrim* and *Except the Lord* are profoundly religious novels, not in any doctrinaire way (unless it is the Protestant belief in direct revelation and salvation by conversion and grace), but rather in "the belief that in life there is something worth doing, and the feeling of it." And, Cary might have added, the *doing* of it. In this sense, *The Horse's Mouth*, for all of Gulley's irreverence, is a religious novel celebrating the source of faith, creative achievement.

The artistic success of the second trilogy, Cary says, "encouraged me to plan a third trilogy, about religion. The subject was fascinating for it is in religion above all that man's imagination has created the most diverse and rich ways of life." [5] This trilogy was to be *The Captive and the Free* which would balance his two studies of the creative artist and the artist as politician with a work on the religious zealot as the artist of the soul; it would complete what he had yet to say about the artist and freedom. Cary indicates that he had contemplated writing a religious trilogy for a long time, "but now I realised that I was too old to be sure of the five or six years which was the minimum time necessary for the work, so the religious novel will have to be a single volume in the third person." [6] The posthumous *The Captive and the Free* is the single volume in the third person which Cary intended as his religious novel.

The Captive and the Free has as its center religion, not as dogma, though dogma is involved in the problem of faith healing, but as a fundamental question of faith in God. The issue is clearly drawn between the rational faith of the Anglican curate Syson and the intuitional faith of the faith healer Preedy, but Cary does not take sides. As in all of his novels, objectivity in presenting convincingly opposing sides in the war of ideas keeps him from taking sides and intruding on the narrative. [7] As Lord Cecil suggests, though Syson "is the more virtuous and intelligent man of the two, and his [Syson's] own final views are stated with sympathy," yet "Preedy's reli-

gion is the real thing," and Syson "is wrong in thinking
Preedy a fraud." In fact, Cecil continues, Syson's views
at the end are close to Cary's own, but Cary was "vigi-
lantly careful to give no hints of this in the book"
(page 7).

Cary's own religious views are succinctly summed up
for us by Cecil in his introduction to *The Captive and
the Free:*

> Cary was a profoundly religious spirit of that intensely
> individual and protestant kind which cannot find fulfillment
> in any corporate body; he had to carve out his creed by him-
> self and for himself. Brought up as an orthodox Anglican, he
> lost all religious faith in early manhood to find a new one in
> mature life. . . . experience had convinced him that man's
> apprehension of beauty and of human love was inexplicable
> on any purely rational or materialist terms. It was proof
> of some transcendental spiritual reality with which a
> man must relate himself harmoniously if he is to find satis-
> faction [page 7].

This summary of Cary's religious views is borne out by
Cary himself in an unpublished essay on his religious history. "It was almost entirely through the aesthetic experience that I came to a true faith," [8] he wrote. While at Oxford his study of Blake profoundly influenced his
thinking:

> I think, indeed, Blake, whom I read and studied at this time,
> had more effect on my idea of the world, for he introduced
> me into a highly complex universe where what is called the
> material is entirely dissolved into imaginative construction
> and states of feeling, where matter, mind and emotion, be-
> come simply different aspects of one reality. [9]

From his understanding of aesthetics and his study of
Blake, Cary found the basis for religious faith in the "formal constructions of art made up of the primitive sensations of colour and sound, the primitive institutions of
love, and truth." Thus, to Cary man's apprehension of

beauty, love, and truth (all aspects of one reality) is inexplicable except on spiritual grounds, because the pure contemplation of beauty has no practical or material value: "I felt it and reacted to it. That is to say, it had the force of a conversion." [10] Lord Cecil, who knew Cary well, says, "He did not hold this as a mere pious opinion. It burned within him, an intuitive conviction as strong as that of Preedy." [11]

The issue between Syson's rational faith and Preedy's intuitive faith turns on the fundamental problem of the existence of evil and injustice in the world: if God is Almighty and at the same time all good, why is there evil and injustice in the world? Preedy, explaining his views to Syson, says, "without freedom of moral choice, there can be neither good nor evil in man. If God did not permit man to do evil he could neither do nor know goodness, he could not know God, which is the greatest happiness, an achievement of man's soul. It is because of man's wickedness that evil is done in the world, and to cure that wickedness there is still God's miracle of grace offered freely to us all" (page 281). Syson, at this point mechanically defending orthodoxy, answers, "God could stop all that evil if he liked and still leave man free to know good and evil. . . . I say that a God who does that [allows evil] would be a devil" (page 282). Syson insists that God cannot do miracles, for "if he can do miracles, why doesn't he do them? Why doesn't he stop all the misery and injustice?" (page 281). Preedy's answer is that God does miracles, but man must have sufficient faith in miracles. Hooper, the journalist, speaking for Preedy, says, "Either God has power to abolish evil or he hasn't, and if he hasn't then he isn't God, in fact there isn't any God" (page 54). It is on this dilemma, for which he has no orthodox answer, that Syson loses his faith: "I had believed that I was free, a free soul serving freely the truth that alone gives freedom" (page 283), but because his orthodoxy will not permit him to believe in miracles, he comes to the conclusion, "there is no freedom—there is no God. We are all simply robots, machines, pushed about by mechanical forces" (page 283).

Syson, though he remains convinced to the end that Preedy is a fraud and a hypocrite, is converted to a faith in God who can do miracles. He receives a letter from a woman whose child had died while Preedy attempted a cure: " 'I know now,' she wrote, 'that you were right, and God could not save my poor child. But still you were wrong too for he can do miracles. He has done one with me, for he has given me forgiveness and peace' " (page 284). It is this letter which converts Syson: "when I read her letter, I was suddenly moved to understand the thing that had stood before my eyes all my life, as wide as the world, as high as the sky, the thing I had repeated a thousand times in prayers and in sermons, without understanding, the miracle of God's love in the world" (page 284). Syson, the captive of his orthodoxy, becomes one of the free by accepting and understanding the contingency of freedom, injustice.

But what is the truth about Preedy—is he a charlatan whose "cures" can be explained on rational grounds? Cary leaves the answer ambiguous for the same reason he leaves unresolved the question in *Aissa Saved* of whether or not prayer and sacrifice can bring the rain—the answer is not essential to the central theme and indeed would confuse it, and to resolve the question one way or the other would destroy the detachment of the author in the battle of ideas. Whether Preedy's "miracles" can be explained rationally, as Syson believes, or whether they are real evidence of God's will and mercy, as Preedy believes, Syson's conversion and Preedy's faith-healing powers arise from the same source, an intuitional faith in God.

Preedy's conversion came as a result of his love affair with Alice Rodker. He freely admits he seduced and then deserted her when she became pregnant, yet he is convinced that their love was "a thing given by God, for a proof of his love for them and all men" (page 94). He believes God sent her to him that he might save her soul and his own through love, "that here had been a miracle of grace, to prove that miracles could happen" (page 94). He now considers it his mission to bring Alice back to God. Syson thinks Preedy a hypocrite who is merely satisfying his sexual passions under the guise of saving Alice's soul. This conflict of views becomes the basis for the Preedy-Syson slander case which Preedy wins because Alice perjures herself. She denies that Preedy was the father of her child.

The fact of Preedy's paternity is denied, but as in the Pincomb-Maufe case in *Not Honour More*, the truth and the facts are not necessarily the same. Alice is motivated by "contempt and defiance. . . . it seemed to her that lying was just what these people had asked for. It was the only proper answer to their attempt to tear out of her things that were the most private in her life" (page 139). Alice's defiance is the measure of her freedom, for the truth—her love for Preedy—would be distorted and made false by the public and by the press who are not interested in the truth but only in the facts which would ruin Preedy.

Though Alice contributes to Preedy's downfall by trying to stop him from attempting to heal any more dying children, she returns to him freely at the end when he is ill. She returns to him, not as a penitent sinner whose soul is lost, but as a free woman understanding and accepting the injustice done to her. Like Sara and Nina, Alice is a prisoner of grace, captive of her responsibility as a woman but freed by her forgiveness and understanding: when Hooper and Joanna ask her to come with them, she says, "But I came to look after him. I've got to look after him —no one else is doing it. And he's really ill" (page 313). Her understanding of what she must do is a kind of conversion, a renewal of faith in her love for Preedy and her duty to him: "She looked at the pair with a new expression, a new realisation came into her face. . . . 'You needn't worry about me,' she said. 'I'm all right. I can take it. I've got straight again and I can take anything' " (page 313). And when the newspaper photographers break into the room to take her picture, giving her the kind of publicity she has feared and tried to avoid, "she tossed her head at them, with the universal gesture of the person who defies the world, the glance of a free soul" (page 314).

Much of the narrative is concerned with the Press and the characters associated with Rideout newspapers—particularly old Kate Rideout, her daughter Joanna, and Harry Hooper. The power struggle within the *Argus* board of directors is secondary to the central situation, the Syson-Preedy conflict. However, the narrative emphasis on the press provides a framework within which the Syson-Preedy case is given universal significance, and it reinforces the main theme, the captive and the free. All those connected with the "free" Press—not only the owners and the members of the board of directors, the editors and the reporters, but also the public itself—are the captives. Thus, the controversy between Syson and Preedy and the relationship between Alice Rodker and Preedy are closely intertwined thematically with the narrative frame involving the "factual" reporting of the Preedy-Syson case.

As Mrs. Davin states in her editorial note to *The Captive and the Free*, Cary "had twice before attempted to write a novel with this title and this theme" (page 9). The two earlier versions, from which the final version evolved, give greater emphasis to the newspaper aspect of the narrative. The first version is written from the point of view (in the third person) of a young newspaper reporter who is the prototype of Hooper:

Young Joint, reporter for the Post Gazetteer, was sent off in a hurry to Cliffam, a small Sussex town. There had been a row after a coroner's inquest, a local faith healer had been assaulted. The young man had hoped for a railway smash in Yorkshire, he had done well on a description of a fire. He looked so disconcerted at the Cliffam arrangement that his chief, amused, said shortly, "It's not my fault—it's the old woman. She wants to give this faith-healing stuff a 'run'."

The old woman was Mrs. Rideout, widow of the late owner, and still owner of one-third of the shares.[12]

Transitional to the second version of *The Captive and the Free* is a new beginning which focuses on Kate Rideout:

None of us was surprised to see that Aunt Kate Rideout had taken up with a new prophet. She had a religious fit every two or three years. We were only relieved to know that this was not a Yoga or a nudist. There was a time just after the war when she proposed to turn the family house into a nudist centre for Europe. Visitors would find her in a drawing room walking about stark naked smoking one of her enormous brown cigarettes, and eager to persuade them that nudism was the secret of health and joy, brotherhood and peace.[13]

The tone of the narration, however, is ironic and skeptical rather than detached and impersonal.

In the second version of *The Captive and the Free* Ann, Kate Rideout's daughter, has been married but is now divorced; she has a child, named Sukey, who is dying from a fatal disease. Kate takes Sukey to Preedy, and Sukey is "cured." As a result Ann becomes a faithful follower of Preedy and falls in love with him.[14] Cary obviously rejected this scheme as being too contrived, but he retained the relationship between Ann and Hooper in this version and developed it as a parallel to the Alice-Preedy relationship in the final version. He retained the element of personal involvement by the Rideouts in Preedy's career through Kate Rideout's illness, her fear of death, and Joanna's concern for Alice, but shifted the narrative focus to an impersonal level by using Hooper as a central point of view and by emphasizing the objective role of the press in the Preedy-Syson controversy.

As in *Not Honour More* Cary explores the paradox that the facts are only a partial view of reality and that the

truth may be distorted by the facts because of the discrepancy between appearance and reality. At the end of
the novel Hooper, defending the role of the Press to
Joanna, says, "We have the facts—facts don't lie" (page
315). But Joanna answers, "Of course they can lie. If you
pick them out in bits. And they're a lie if you use that
picture—a wicked, cruel lie against that poor man" (page
315). The "fact" that Preedy hit Alice, "proven" by a
photograph, would distort the truth of the final relationship between Alice and Preedy. Hooper himself knows
the truth:

he could describe the girl Rodker as really the stronger party;
as a person of remarkable character who had come back to
Preedy simply because it seemed to be the right thing to do
and to whom that black eye was of no importance whatever.
Who had perhaps even originally been more seducer than
seduced. Though, of course, he could not exonerate Preedy
[page 316].

But Hooper is the captive of his own ambition and of the
public he serves:

No, there was only one story here—the poor little girl
seduced and ruined by a parson who then proceeds to murder
her baby, who has such power over her still that he recalls
her to his side and beats her up as a reward. And the poor
little victim, besotted with love or terror, takes it. One could
suggest perhaps that she likes being beaten; always a popular
line [page 317].

Hooper, as a central point of view, provides the link
with Preedy, for he takes Preedy's side, joins the mission's
committee, and at times acts as Preedy's spokesman. But
he does not really believe in Preedy; he is without faith.
Hooper is basically motivated by the desire for power in
the struggle for control of the Rideout Press. He says he
believes in freedom, but he is the captive of his ambition.
He pursues Joanna as part of his struggle for power and
success; but when he wins her, he is the captive of his
pride which prevents him from accepting the situation;

when Joanna tells him she is pregnant, he is furious with her, thinking himself trapped by his own driving ambition. Though he tells her he would rather shoot himself than marry her, they are soon married; it is this part of their relationship that Cary would obviously have developed and clarified in revision, for the reader is unprepared for it.

If Hooper's attitude toward Joanna remains ambivalent and unresolved, except on the calculated level of ambition, Joanna's love for him is clear and straightforward: she is, as Cary says, "captive of her fear of loneliness— isolation. of being cut-off. . . . She realises mother's loneliness and it terrifies her. . . . She is attracted to Hooper by his apparent confidence and faith, his independence." [15] Thus, Joanna provides a contrasting parallel to Alice Rodker: both are attracted to men of power, confidence, and independence; but whereas Hooper's freedom is only apparent and his faith nonexistent, Preedy's freedom and faith are real. Both accept their men in the end; but whereas Alice freely returns to Preedy, perceiving her responsibility to him and thus paradoxically gaining her freedom, Joanna, though she has fallen in love with Hooper, acquiesces to his unromantic proposal of marriage ("It would strengthen my position on the *Argus*") because she is still the captive of her fear of loneliness.

Joanna in the beginning is skeptical of Preedy while Hooper defends him and apparently believes him. But in the end it is Joanna who defends Preedy against Hooper and his submission to the demands of the "free" press. Yet her "conversion" is not a true intuitional faith but a confusion of mind:

Had she joined up, did she really believe? It seemed to her that she had passed only from prejudice against Preedy into a strong but vague feeling that, after all, he might be a great, an extraordinary person; with mysterious powers. But this discovery had merely added to the violent confusion in her mind. She had changed that empty darkness in which she had felt like a creature imprisoned in nothingness, to a darkness

full of mysterious shapes and noises whose meaning was in-
comprehensible [page 180].

Joanna's conversion is motivated by a sense of guilt because she lacks faith (Hooper seems to believe), but her
confusion of mind is genuine. Cary sought to relate it to
the revolution of ideas in modern times and probably he
would have developed this point in revision: "It is the
confusion of modern life, the sudden changes, the appearance of new forces that has overwhelmed the crowd.
(Like Joanna) They are lost, shrunk and bewildered with
nonsense. Science *and* religion." [16]

If Joanna's conversion represents a confusion of mind,
her mother's support of Preedy represents a confusion
of values. As skeptical about Preedy as her daughter, Kate
Rideout originally supports him as a means of increasing
the circulation of the *Argus,* but her fear of death and
her loneliness cause her to seek a private meeting with
Preedy in the hope of a cure. After the "Clench miracle,"
she joins Preedy's Mission as a hedge against the possibility that there might be something in this faith-healing
business and that Preedy might be able to effect a cure.
Her "conversion" is devoid of real faith, but she is
"cured," or at least she convinces herself she is well.
However, three months later she dies of an "incurable"
disease, cancer of the spinal cord, putting her final faith
in medical science.

Kate Rideout's death precipitates a financial and political crisis for the board of directors of the *Argus* which
parallels the crisis facing the governing committee of the
Pant's Road Mission brought about by the inquest into
the death of the girl Ada Rollwright whom Preedy has
been trying to cure. In contrast to the materialistic concern of the governing committee is the crisis of faith
reached by both Syson and Preedy at this point. Both
Syson and Preedy resolve their doubts by a renewal of
faith in God: Syson through his understanding of "the
miracle of God's love in the world" and Preedy, in the

middle of a sermon, by his belief that God has sent him a direct sign of the truth when the sun breaks through the clouds.

Cary wrote in an unpublished note, *"Relig. central. Start & end there. Fundamental. The Truth (the free)."* [17] In the final version Cary made the religious theme more central by beginning with Syson, thus focusing from the start on the conflict between Syson and Preedy rather than on the parallel conflict within the Rideout Press. That the novel ends with Hooper rather than Syson, thus placing final emphasis on the "truth" as reported in the newspapers, is probably something Cary would have changed in revision. Though Cary did not bring the novel quite full circle, the religious theme does come full circle in the two parallel and nearly simultaneous religious crises of Syson and Preedy and the renewal of faith which makes them free. Hooper's crisis of conscience at the end must be viewed as part of the same theme: he is the captive of the facts from which Syson, in his rationalism, had to free himself before he could believe again, and which Preedy had to deny so that he could be free to believe.

Cary is clearly on the side of the free against the captives in all his novels. The comedy of freedom is the love, joy, beauty, and happiness of life itself. Paradoxically, the tragedy of freedom is the injustice that exists in life as a necessary condition of freedom. The greatest freedom is achieved in creative activity, whether in politics, religion, or art, but with creativity comes responsibility for evil as well as good. The free are captives of their captivity which makes them free, but as Cary notes, "The Free *perceive* their captivity which is the conditions [sic] of their creative life." [18] To understand one's captivity is to be free.

NOTES

CHAPTER I

1. James M. Osborn Collection of Joyce Cary Manuscripts, Box Number 321, Typescript version of a letter addressed, not in Cary's hand, to Mark Schorer. The manuscript collection has been catalogued by Professor Andrew Wright. The catalogue, *Hand List of the Joyce Cary Manuscripts of James M. Osborn Deposited in the Bodleian Library*, Oxford (1958), lists the contents of each manuscript box. It is an invaluable guide to the collection. The Joyce Cary manuscript collection will hereafter be referred to as the Osborn Collection.

2. Osborn Collection, Box Number 1, Autograph version of letter addressed to Mr. Hughes.

3. Joyce Cary, *First Trilogy*, p. x.

4. Barbara Hardy, "Form in Joyce Cary's Novels," *Essays in Criticism*, IV, 184.

CHAPTER II

1. Osborn Collection, Box Number 326, Holograph version of a letter in a paper folder labeled "Notes on Trilogy for U. S. A. Letter to E. L." in large folder labeled "Notes on Books for Harpers." Hereafter referred to as letter to E. L.

1. Joyce Cary, "The Way a Novel Gets Written," *Harper's*, CC, 88.

3. Joyce Cary, "My First Novel," *Listener*, p. 638.

4. Osborn Collection, Box Number 2, Holograph sheet. There are many canceled lines in this passage. In the manuscript versions of *Aissa Saved* the missionaries are named Cole, but Cary changed the name to Carr because "there were several Coles, on the West Coast, about that time" (Osborn Collection, Box Number 1, short, one page Autograph version of a letter addressed to Mr. Hughes, not the same letter referred to previously).

5. Osborn Collection, Box Number 2, Holograph sheet 1,

in paper folder labeled in Mrs. Davin's hand "Draft of novel's opening, in which Ojo goes alone to Yanrin, finds Aissa in the Zonga and, with Musa's help, rescues her from the mob." Mrs. Winifred Davin is literary advisor to the Joyce Cary estate.

6. Osborn Collection, Box Number 1.

7. Osborn Collection, Box Number 2, Holograph sheet 1, in paper folder labeled in Mrs. Davin's hand "Another opening of the novel in which Aissa is called Baju. She has already made one expedition to Yanrin, and this is mainly concerned with her first communion."

8. Andrew Wright, *Joyce Cary: A Preface to His Novels*, p. 75. Professor Wright suggests that Aissa's Christianity is understood in exclusively female and even sexual terms.

9. Osborn Collection, Box Number 1, Autograph version of letter to Mr. Hughes.

10. Ibid.

11. Joyce Cary, *Aissa Saved*, p. 113. Subsequent page references are to this Carfax edition.

12. Osborn Collection, Box Number 1, Typescript sheet 101 in bundle labeled "Aissa."

13. Osborn Collection, Box Number 2, Holographic sheets 11, 12.

14. Osborn Collection, Box Number 2, Holographic sheet 12.

15. See Cary's note on this: "Essentials of end Aissa moved by love of Jesus demanding all gives all i.e. *she gives up herself*. The purpose of saving people not Aissa's (but the leaders, Mokato etc)." Osborn Collection, Box Number 2, Holographic sheet. (Italics are Cary's.)

16. Osborn Collection, Box Number 1, Autograph version of letter to Mr. Hughes.

17. Note Ali's acceptance of the idea of witches, whether or not they have power over rain (p. 88).

18. In an unpublished novel, *Daventry*, written in the 1920's, Daventry, a young district officer in Nigeria on his first tour of duty, is the prototype of Bewsher, a romantic man of action seeking adventure. His superior officer, Crampton, is the prototype of Rudbeck, the visionary builder of roads:

So when Crampton, seeking his vision, came to Daventry, and said "I want you to make a road through the pagan division . . . ," Daventry saw the vision too, but a vision of much more certain outline and colour. Crampton's was a bright vague dream of civilization, Daventry's a clear picture of himself, working, daring, a pioneer in boots and breeches, riding on a pony, with a revolver in his belt. [Osborn Collection, Box Number 107, Holograph sheet.]

19. Osborn Collection, Box Number 3, Holograph sheet.

20. Joyce Cary, *An American Visitor*, pp. 7–8. Subsequent page references are to this Carfax edition.

21. Wright, *Joyce Cary*, p. 60.

22. Osborn Collection, Box Number 8, Typescript sheet 1.

23. Osborn Collection, Box Number 6, Holograph sheet.

24. Cary, *An American Visitor*, p. 215. Note also that Dobson ironically foreshadows the ending when he preaches: "The veriest savage hesitates to kill the man who comes unarmed and in the name of friendship" (p. 219).

25. Osborn Collection, Box Number 6, Holograph paper folder labeled "Characters, Plan, etc."

26. Ibid.

27. Osborn Collection, Box Number 6, Typescript sheet 305.

28. Robert Bloom, *The Indeterminate World: A Study of the Novels of Joyce Cary*. Bloom himself seems ambivalent in the attitude he should take toward this quality. While on the one hand praising it as the source of the strength and vitality of Cary's novels, on the other hand (when he condemns it as the source of Cary's failure) he speaks disparagingly of "the vice of objectivity" and indeterminateness which "do significant damage when they act upon the trilogies as wholes" (pp. 41, 42). It would seem that Professor Bloom simply begs the question rather than proves his "thesis."

29. Joyce Cary, *The African Witch*, p. 9. Subsequent page references are to this Carfax edition.

30. This early work may or may not be the original sketch Cary refers to.

31. In a note on Aladé, Cary writes, "Themes. Nationalist feeling & its destruction. Fear etc that produces it." The note continues, "Theme is—the desire to create—thwarted by direct role etc—the soul of nationalism—the desire for independence, for power, and to create." (Osborn Collection, Box Number 96, Holograph sheet.) Louis Aladai's nationalism is tempered by his Europeanization.

32. Osborn Collection, Box Number 96, Paper folder labeled "Aladé cursing the whites. 10."

33. Osborn Collection, Box Number 96, Holograph sheets 1–3. Contains cancellations.

34. In an early version of the novel's ending Judy Coote leaves Nigeria and later marries an Oxford don, settling down to motherhood and obscurity! (Osborn Collection, Box Number 10, Holograph sheet in paper folder labeled "14 end.") In a later version the marriage to the Oxford don is "annulled" by the author's simple method of canceling it out. This version ends, significantly, with Judy teaching English to Tom, thus ending with a note of hope for the future; the final chapter of the published version was added later. Cf. Osborn Collection, Box Number 11, Holograph sheet.

35. Osborn Collection, small, blue, unlabeled "Memo Book" notebook.

36. Mark Schorer, *New York Times Book Review* (October 7, 1951), p. 1. Such major novelists as Joyce and Woolf were fully committed to the importance of the immediacy of experience; it is their technique that differs from Cary's.

37. Joyce Cary, *Mister Johnson*, pp. 7, 10. Subsequent page references are to this Carfax edition.

38. Osborn Collection, Holograph sheets in paper folder labeled "Mr. Johnson" in large red folder labeled "M.S. Sketches in Jackets." Contains cancellations.

39. Ibid.

40. Wright, *Joyce Cary*, p. 85, suggests that Johnson's murder of Gollup is his last and greatest act. Such an interpretation of the murder as the creative act of a free man ignores the reality of events which drove Johnson to murder; the destructive element of Johnson's romanticism destroys him as surely as it destroys Conrad's Lord Jim. Like Lord Jim, Johnson's freedom exists only in the realm of illusion and imagination.

41. Osborn Collection, Box Number 24, Typescript sheet in package labeled "Rough Copy of Mr. Johnson." Contains cancellations.

CHAPTER III

1. Joyce Cary, *Castle Corner*, p. 5. Subsequent page references are to this Carfax edition.

2. Osborn Collection, Box Number 21, beige folder labeled "They want to be happy," Holographic sheets. These sheets contain outline notes on the series, giving dates, characters and historical events. One of them gives the individual titles "Castle Corner," "Over the Top," and "Green Jerusalem" for the series, which is to be a "Scheme in three books." A fourth volume is not referred to here, but in this original scheme Cary intended to carry the events in *Castle Corner* to 1908 or 1910: "1st book . . . Story ending in 1908 (10) with murder." Other sheets briefly outlined the major events to be covered by the other two volumes: "2nd book. Over the top. Suffragettes. *Irish Civil War*. Politics. Parliament Act, War, Treaty. Russian Revolution." "3rd book. Gen. strike. election of 1931. Peace Ballot. League. Emergence of planning idea. Young people."

3. Wright, *Joyce Cary*, pp. 32, 66.

4. The one character in *Castle Corner*, James Slatter, who consistently and single-mindedly seeks to get Castle Corner and to whom the castle is of symbolic value, does not acquire it in the projected scheme of this series. As representative of the new commercial class of property owners, he is thwarted from gaining this symbol of the old order at the very beginning by an ironic twist: Felix Corner, who is expected to inherit Castle Corner and who would sell to Slatter, does not inherit it. Slatter's hopes of eventually getting the castle are as futile as John Chass Corner's hopes of a financial miracle.

5. Osborn Collection, Box Number 114, Holograph sheet in green folder labeled "Working."

6. Ibid.

7. Ibid.

8. Osborn Collection, Box Number 105, Holograph letter included in beige folder.

9. Osborn Collection, Box Number 21, paper folder labeled "11 The Inquest etc."; also an earlier version in Box Number 17 in folder labeled "Castle Corner New Chapters."

10. Though Cary meant to create characters and leave them to act, he was predominantly concerned with "universal *political* questions" and their answers (*Castle Corner*, p. 7). For example, the many characters introduced in the first chapter of *Castle Corner* and their actions seem intended to illustrate the various implications of the Irish land laws as they affect the large landowners like the Corners, the Irish

peasants like the Foys, and the land speculators like Slatter who were the only ones who really profited from the change. The novel begins effectively with Old John Chass Corner saying prayers at meal time; Old John represents the old order, but he is dying as the old order is dying, and with his death the old order dies although his son John Chass struggles on to keep it alive. The tradition of saying prayers at meals ends with the death of the old man, and this becomes an illustration of the change that occurs when the new generation takes over. Felix Corner goes off to Africa to make his fortune, and the scene shifts to Africa and its revolution in the second chapter. The Foys are individualized as characters, but their actions are intended to illustrate the plight of the Irish peasants, the land wars, the emigration to America, and later through Manus Foy the whole upheaval over home rule and the Irish nationalist movement. Sukey Egan and later Bridget Foy, though again individualized and developed as characters, are intended to represent the servant class retaining their own folkways but also remaining loyal to the old order which they serve. Philip Feenix in contrast to Cleeve Corner, who escapes from the decaying world of Annish into the changing world of Oxford and London, remains and is defeated by the revolution he serves although he wanted the freedom Cleeve achieves through his education; thus, Philip becomes an illustration of that failure to adjust to the changing times, an embittered romantic who loses all his illusions, takes to drink, cynically marries, and finally kills himself. Mary Corner, in contrast to Helen Pynsant the modern emancipated woman, is intended to represent the old family order in which she as wife and mother manages the household and raises the children but leaves politics to the men; though she is a stabilizing center at the castle, she is ineffective in influencing and controlling the changes that occur around her because her concept of happiness belongs to the old order. Thus, though Cary does create characters and leaves them to act, they act according to his over-all plan "as illustrations of general laws." (*Castle Corner*, p. 8.)

11. Osborn Collection, notes in Boxes Numbers 21 and 114.

12. Of the characters in *Castle Corner* whose lives are continued and developed in *Over the Top* and *Green Jerusalem*, Cock Jarvis, Stella, and Bridget are the major characters, and Hatto is developed more fully. Of the new charac-

ters introduced, Delia Baskett is the most prominent. She represents the new generation of women; she is emancipated like Helen Pynsant (she is a businesswoman and involved in politics, thus her friendship with Cleeve), but like Mary Corner, she finds her happiness in marriage and motherhood. She combines successfully the values of the old world and the new: "Delia goes out to the world with rich sympathy and excitement—for things as well as people and ideas. She is alive all the time and greedy of life, for others as well as herself. . . . She is baffled or angered by cynical or mean people, she can't understand why they should make themselves unhappy or deal in unhappiness—when it is just as easy to be generous." (Osborn Collection, Box Number 20, Holographic note in paper folder labeled "Delia Baskett. Beginning.") This quality of sympathy and her Quaker upbringing lead her to attempt a reconciliation between Stella and Cleeve even though she is at the time in love with Cleeve. The younger generation begins to take over against their elders—Mavis and Dick, Stella's children, lose their happiness because they do not change; Finian finds happiness but breaks Cleeve's heart because of his ideas which are a denial of all that he values. Thus Cary continues the pattern established in *Castle Corner:* the young people who have their roots in the previous generation become part of the revolution that changes the old way of life and they in turn become the tradition against which their children rebel. Felix Corner, a rationalist and socialist, helped create the social revolution which ruins his family and which in turn separates him from his son Cleeve, who becomes a part of the new order which hardens into tradition and against which his son Finian rebels. Cary successfully creates the pattern of change, but in so doing loses the pattern of art which would give form to it.

13. Osborn Collection, notes in Boxes Numbers 21 and 105.

14. Osborn Collection, Box Number 105 and, particularly, black loose leaf notebook labeled "C. J. [Cock Jarvis] Data."

15. Cary, *The African Witch*, p. 11. Cary did not avoid entirely the African setting in *Castle Corner.*

16. *Arabella* begins: "The twins Arabella and Charles were left orphans at the age of two, upon the doorstep of Miss Ellen Ankle. Their parents were unknown and probably disreputable. They were babies of surprising beauty. All Miss

Ankle's relations at once advised her to send them to the workhouse; and especially her brother in law and trustee Professor Hoopey, who had always looked after her interests." But Professor Hoopey is won over by the children, or rather by the idea of giving them a modern education, and Ellen adopts them. Suddenly the children are grown up and are concerned about careers: Charles wants to be a poet, but he is worried about money and tries to get his sister married off to a wealthy man. Arabella goes her own way and gets a job as secretary to Mr. Basham who is president of the Junior Federation of Progress and Liberty, and who is an enthusiast in radical politics and a world traveler. They go to France, Germany, and Russia where they become enthusiastic about communism. When the United States is conquered by the Bolshevists, they travel there. The description of Bolshevized America is crude political satire: "The Bolshevist conquest of America was welcomed not only by the communist organizations; by the architects and engineers who wanted work and the professors of political economy who wished to practice their themes on a living model; but by the majority of the people who thought the old Roosevelt dollar was too dear and that a majority of the other people wanted shooting. They said that there weren't enough dollars in the pay envelope and too many in the bankers' vaults. The rebellion therefore which sent the dollar down to two cents and all the bankers to the electric chair gave general pleasure." One need only compare this with Orwell's *Nineteen Eighty-Four*, if not with the complex mood of the United States during the depression and the early years of the New Deal, to recognize the naïveté of its conception as satiric fantasy, and one need only compare it with *Aissa Saved* and *An American Visitor* to be surprised by the weakness of the writing. In the predictable end Arabella converts the bourgeois-hunter Mungo to bourgeois values and the novel ends with a long speech by Basham denouncing communism. (Osborn Collection, Box Number 98, Typescript sheets.)

Marta, with its beginning description of a London slum street, evokes a definite mood by its realistic detail:

Occam Street in London S.E. does not look like a slum but it is the worst in that neighbourhood, full of slums. It is a long straight street, forty feet wide; flanked by long straight rows of neat two story houses. These houses were built in 1902 for artisans of good class. . . . But Occam Street is a slum because it is full of slum people. . . .

One afternoon in the June of 1935, such an intruder was seen advancing slowly down Occam Street. She was an old woman bent forward crookedly, so that she seemed to have a one sided hump. Her knees were [bent] over like an old cab horse's, and she limped on both feet. Her gait was a kind of shuffling roll, which affected her whole head and body so that her rusty old black hat, a kind of pancake of filthy crape, jumped on her bald head, and her dirty black skirts which seemed four times too large for her skeleton body, so that they hung upon her projecting buttocks in folds and festoons of cloth, were jerked up and down in the ludicrous manner affected by low comedians when they imitate a mincing girl.

Marta collapses in the street and is discovered to be Lady Martha Portlock, a famous beauty of the 1880's but now an old and ugly woman. The second chapter goes back to her childhood:

When Marta was a little girl with a round face, very pale straight hair, a bulging forehead and thick short legs, she would often hear words like pleasure, enjoyment, happiness. . . .

Marta paid no attention to these words. She was too busy with her own affairs, rushing about on some errand or other, playing and fighting with her friends. To her, grown ups were like part of the weather; elements far above her head and uncontrollable which upset or furthered her plans in a capricious manner. . . .

Marta was often in trouble, but she forgot her wrongs before others could forgive them, and though of course, untidy, careless, a liar and pilferer, and not great[ly] affectionate, she was so happy that she was greatly beloved . . . [Osborn Collection, Box Number 111, Typescript sheets.]

The rest of the manuscript continues with her life. Professor Wright has sufficiently outlined in detail the main story of this fragmentary novel (cf. Wright, *Joyce Cary*, pp. 52–54). Cary's obvious intention was to recount Marta's life to explain why she ends up a broken old woman in Occam Street, but the manuscript breaks off before that point. The writing is obviously better than that in *Arabella* although it is not as good as the writing in *Aissa Saved* or *An American Visitor*. One must remember, however, that Cary's method of constant revision would undoubtedly have resulted in further improvements in the writing of *Marta* whereas *Arabella* is a completed manuscript which Cary sent to his agent.

CHAPTER IV

1. Wright, *Joyce Cary*, p. 17.
2. Joyce Cary, *A House of Children*, p. 7. Subsequent page references are to this Carfax edition.
3. Osborn Collection, Box Number 19, Holograph sheets 1 and 2, containing many cancellations.
4. Osborn Collection, Box Number 19, Holograph sheet, containing many cancellations.
5. Joyce Cary, *Charley Is My Darling*, p. 8. Subsequent page references are to this Carfax edition.
6. Anthony West, "Books: Footloose and Fancy-Free," *New Yorker*, XXXVI (April 30, 1960), 170–76.
7. *Mister Tottenham, Victim of Love*, an unpublished but completed novel probably written during the 1930's, is the story of a young boy of eight, Johnny Brant, who is teased and bullied by his classmates at school and by his brother Harry. Johnny, who is taunted with the nickname Mister Tottenham, is a sensitive boy who suffers from a sense of inferiority and injustice. In compensation his behavior is violent, earning him the disapproval of grown-ups and the bullying of his contemporaries. The opening scene illustrates his rage at the injustice of being blamed for the quarrel with his brother Harry who started it:

It seemed to Johnny that the injustice from which he was suffering entitled him to let himself go, and therefore he was growing more furious and desperate every minute. On the second landing he suddenly tore himself out of nurse's hands and threw himself downstairs. He meant to kill somebody. However he was brought within a few steps against the balusters, and Nurse, infuriated by the fright he had given her, pounced on him and shook him. [Osborn Collection, Box Number 114, p. 4 of Typescript.]

Johnny is driven to commit suicide by the teasing and bullying of his schoolmates. The inquest jury, however, brings in a verdict of death by misadventure to save the parents' feelings, who believed they loved him, and because the jury could not believe a young boy who was so loved could commit suicide. Thus the title is ironic.

Johnny Brant is no Charley Brown, a born creator, and there is no evidence that *Tottenham* was used by Cary as a basis for *Charley Is My Darling*. However, it does indicate Cary's concern with the complex world of childhood in which happiness and unhappiness, love and hate, comedy and tragedy, lie so close to the surface of life and are the directly felt emotions of experience. In *Tottenham* Cary relied on a sensational plot, but in *Charley Is My Darling* and *A House of Children* Cary learned to reveal a child's world through development of character.

8. Osborn Collection, Box Number 26, Holograph sheet in paper folder labeled "Charley. Plot & theme."

9. Osborn Collection, Box Number 28, Holograph sheet.

10. Osborn Collection, Box Number 26, Holograph sheet in paper folder labeled "Charley. Plot & theme."

11. Osborn Collection, Box Number 28, Holograph sheet.

12. Osborn Collection, Box Number 31, note on front-cover of paper folder labeled "H. of C. Notes etc."

13. Osborn Collection, Box Number 31, Holograph sheet in paper folder labeled "Characters."

14. Osborn Collection, Box Number 30, Typescript sheet in paper folder labeled "H of C. Beginning. I." There are some cancellations in this passage. The manuscript version continues as in the published text: "Of course we heard nothing of the other side of the old Empire."

15. Osborn Collection, Box Number 31, Holograph sheets in folder numbered "11. Summer 99." Italics mine, for those passages which do not appear in the published text, except that the word "felt" is underlined in the manuscript version.

16. Osborn Collection, Box Number 31, Holograph sheet in folder labeled "Characters."

17. Osborn Collection, Box Number 31, paper folder numbered "11. Summer 99." Italics mine, corresponding to the words rejected in the published text.

18. Osborn Collection, Box Number 30, Holograph sheet in paper folder numbered "5."

19. Ibid.

CHAPTER V

1. Joyce Cary, *Herself Surprised*, p. 7. Subsequent page references are to this Carfax edition.

2. Cary, "The Way a Novel Gets Written," pp. 87, 88, 89.

3. Osborn Collection, Holograph sheet 3 in large brown folder labeled "Lectures." Contains a cancellation.

4. Osborn Collection, Box Number 242, Typescript sheet 8 in envelope labeled "Blurb on Trilogy. For: The Horses Mouth" and sent to his publisher Michael Joseph in December, 1942, or January, 1943, for this envelope contains a letter from the publisher dated January 13, 1943, thanking Cary for the blurb. It is in this blurb that Cary indicated his original intention of ending *The Horse's Mouth* with a newspaper obituary notice of Gulley Jimson's death. The obituary notice is as follows:

Mr. Gulley Jimson, distinguished painter of the nude.

Mr. Jimson's last exhibition in the twenties excited considerable attention and in some quarters high hopes for English painting. His best work at this period of maturity shewed strongly the influence of Renoir. In late years, however, Mr. Jimson devoted himself entirely to murals. The change has been attributed to the loss of a favourite model [Sara], subject of former studies. However this may be, most critics are agreed that the artist's later work, while displaying considerable vigour and plastic invention, does not, in the drier medium give scope for that painterlike brilliance of handling which in his flesh painting surprised and delighted even connoisseurs of the great French school.

Mr. Jimson, for some time before his death, had been in

failing health and lived a very retired life with a few old friends. We understand that one of these intimates, Mr. Robin Alabaster, has written a monograph on the painter's life and work, which may be expected in the spring lists. It is perhaps too early for a final assessment of Jimson's achievement but Mr. Alabaster advances strong arguments to shew that the early reputation, founded on the brilliant handling of the nudes, was well deserved, and will increase with the passage of time. [Osborn Collection, Box Number 242, Typescript sheet 5.]

5. Osborn Collection, Holograph sheets, pp. 1–2 in large brown folder labeled "Notes on Books for Harpers." It could be another version of the letter to "E. L." Contains some cancellations. For a detailed discussion of how the first trilogy evolved, see my article "The Genesis and Development of Joyce Cary's First Trilogy," *PMLA*, LXXVIII (September 1963), 431–39.

6. Ibid., Holograph sheets, p. 2. Contains cancellations.

7. Cary, "The Way a Novel Gets Written," p. 92.

8. Osborn Collection, Box Number 39, Holograph sheets. In some of these notes Cary, perhaps unconsciously, shifts into the first person point of view of his character. This characteristic is observable in other notes, particularly in the notebooks relating to the novels of both trilogies.

9. Osborn Collection, Holograph sheets in unlabeled, marbleized-covered, medium-sized notebook. The variant spellings of Gulley and Wilcher are original variants of their names as characters.

10. Years later in *The Horse's Mouth* she comes to admire herself in that painting, reflecting not only her own self-admiration, but also the advance of public taste which has caught up with impressionism.

11. Osborn Collection, Box Number 33, Holograph sheet.

12. Osborn Collection, Box Number 33, Typescript sheets.

13. Ibid.

14. Ibid.

15. Ibid.

16. Osborn Collection, Box Number 33, Typescript half-sheet. Cf. with pp. 97–98 of published text.

17. Osborn Collection, Box Number 34, Typescript sheet 2.

18. Joyce Cary, *To Be a Pilgrim,* p. 313. Subsequent page references are to this Carfax edition.

19. Osborn Collection, Box Number 39, medium-sized notebook labeled "To be a P."

20. Osborn Collection, unlabeled red, small-sized notebook.

21. Walter Allen, *Joyce Cary,* p. 24.

22. Osborn Collection, unlabeled red, small-sized notebook. An alternative ending to the plan would have Wilcher sent to prison where he dies, unhappy to the end because he cannot be a pilgrim.

23. Osborn Collection, Box Number 42, Holograph sheet.

24. Osborn Collection, Box Number 39, medium-sized notebook labeled "To be a P."

25. Cary, *To Be a Pilgrim,* p. 328. This love of the land and its continuity with history is linked with his love for Sara.

26. Osborn Collection, Box Number 43, Holograph sheet in bundle labeled "Horses Mouth MS."

27. Joyce Cary, *The Horse's Mouth,* p. 11. Subsequent page references are to this Carfax edition. In an early, rejected beginning to *The Horse's Mouth,* though the first person technique is used, the narrator is not Gulley Jimson, but an artist who knew him in his student days in Paris: "Last Year two books were published mentioning a man called Jimson, an artist who had some distinction about ten or fifteen years ago but is now forgotten. I knew Jimson thirty years ago. We were in Paris together, the old Paris of the Fauves, of 1910; and afterwards in London." (Osborn Collection, Box Number 43, Holograph sheet. Contains cancellations.) This rejected beginning in its entirety is included in Wright, *Joyce Cary,* pp. 156–64.

28. In an earlier version of the same opening passage Cary used a different quotation from Blake than the one in the published text: "Where is my cunning bird of Eden. . . ." Although this Blake quotation is related to the theme of "The Fall," it is less immediately relevant to Gulley's flow of thoughts and associations than the one finally chosen. (Osborn Collection, Box Number 41, Holograph sheet in paper folder labeled "MS. *Horse's Mouth* opening found in wire in tray.") See Wright, *Joyce Cary,* pp. 165–73, for identification of the passages from Blake.

29. Osborn Collection, Box Number 43, Holograph sheet

in manuscript bundle labeled "Horse's Mouth MS. & odd pieces."

30. Osborn Collection, Box Number 41, Holograph sheet in paper folder labeled "Horse's Mouth."

31. Ibid.

32. John Burrows and Alex Hamilton, "Joyce Cary," *Writers at Work: The "Paris Review" Interviews*, p. 65.

33. Cary, *The Horse's Mouth*, p. 52. Sexuality and creativity are directly linked in this quotation.

34. Cary, *The Horse's Mouth*, p. 170. In an unpublished note which is related to the original plan for *The Horse's Mouth* Cary wrote, linking God and the artist as creators, "The artist [Moore] seeks to make beauty & lets all else slide. . . . His sense of religion & god—'god is an artist.'" (Osborn Collection, medium sized notebook labeled "P" [Plots].)

35. Cary, *The Horse's Mouth*, p. 241. Originally, Cary's description of the Creation was more explicitly Eve-centered: "The whole flying in the air, the man in the sea, the woman with eight breasts. The whole with a woman's head, swelling itself. . . . Emerging out of the inside of a brain—Gods brain." (Osborn Collection, Box Number 41, paper folder labeled "Description of C." A sketch accompanies this description.)

CHAPTER VI

1. Osborn Collection, Box Number 99, Typescript sheet.

2. Osborn Collection, Box Number 99, Holograph sheets 1 and 2 in paper folder labeled "New beginning. '49." Contains cancellations.

3. Osborn Collection, Box Number 99, Holograph sheets in paper folder labeled "E. M." The "talker" is Doatie Pilcher. Contains cancellations.

4. Osborn Collection, Box Number 59, Holograph sheet 1 in paper folder containing title "Turkish House" on its cover. Contains many cancellations.

5. Osborn Collection, Box Number 59, Holograph sheet 4.

6. Osborn Collection, Box Number 99, Holograph sheet 1

in paper folder labeled "C and F Gye beginning A. 1." Contains many cancellations.

7. Osborn Collection, Box Number 53, Holograph sheet in paper folder labeled "F. J. M. S.—Throw Outs." Contains cancellations.

8. One character common to both versions is Barfoot who in the first version is involved in dubious real estate deals with Lord Drummer and later becomes his enemy, and who in the second version was the nurse of the two sisters but who becomes a real estate owner and agent. In one of the beginnings of this version, a first person account from Hannah's point of view, Hannah is Barfoot's secretary. The third version of *The Captive and the Free*, from evidence of the quality of the paper and the handwriting, is the earliest. However, there is no indication that this version was planned as a trilogy, and it involves an entirely different set of characters from the other two versions, the Taneys, but it does involve the relationship of two sisters, Dorothy and Edith Taney. See Osborn Collection, Box Number 102.

9. Osborn Collection, Box Number 100, Holograph sheet pasted on inside cover of green folder labeled "Characters."

10. Ibid.

11. Osborn Collection, Holograph sheet in black, large-sized looseleaf folder.

12. Osborn Collection, Holograph sheets in medium-sized looseleaf folder labeled "C & F."

13. One projected scheme for the trilogy covers events from the 1870's through the 1930's (Osborn Collection, Box Number 100, Holograph sheet in green folder labeled "Characters"), but another scheme projects events to 1948 (Osborn Collection, Holograph sheet in unlabeled, large-sized, black-covered looseleaf notebook).

14. Osborn Collection, Holograph sheet pasted on inside cover of green folder labeled "Characters."

15. Osborn Collection, Box Number 100, Holograph sheet in black-covered, large-sized looseleaf folder.

16. Ibid.

17. Osborn Collection, Box Number 100, Holograph sheet pasted on inside cover of green folder labeled "Characters."

18. Osborn Collection, Holograph sheet, black-covered, large-sized looseleaf notebook. In this same note Cary indicates that Roberta's life is intended as a summing up in the

third volume of the trilogy; however, this is only a projected plan, and the third volume was not written in this version.

19. Box Number 101 contains a present-tense version of Hannah's life, but it is written in the first person from Hannah's point of view as Barfoot's secretary. The version referred to here is the third-person, past-tense narrative found in Box Number 100.

20. Joyce Cary, *The Moonlight*, p. 9. Subsequent page references are to this Carfax edition.

21. Osborn Collection, Box Number 47, Holograph note in orange-covered, medium-sized notebook labeled "Moon."

22. The "sudden death" of characters is a weakness of plot often found in family chronicles, but here, though still a weakness, it is essential to the central situation, Rose's sacrifice.

23. Osborn Collection, Holograph note in orange-covered, medium-sized notebook labeled "Moon."

24. Osborn Collection, Box Number 47, Holograph note in unlabeled, blue-covered, small-sized notebook.

25. Osborn Collection, Box Number 47, Holograph note in orange-covered, medium-sized notebook labeled "Moon."

26. Osborn Collection, Box Number 47, Holograph sheet in paper folder in envelope labeled "Bits of The Moonlight."

27. Osborn Collection, Box Number 47, Holograph sheet in orange-covered, medium-sized notebook labeled "Moon."

28. Ibid.

29. Ibid.

30. Osborn Collection, Box Number 47, Holograph sheet in paper folder headed "Characters" in envelope labeled "Bits of The Moonlight."

31. Cary, *The Moonlight*, p. 16. Her work, ironically, consists of research on primitive tribal customs.

32. Osborn Collection, Box Number 47, Holograph sheet in paper folder headed "Characters" in envelope labeled "Bits of The Moonlight."

33. Cary, *The Moonlight*, p. 150. In this same passage the Victorian plush curtains droop "with crimson folds like the walls of some immense womb." The image evokes a feeling of revulsion in Amanda, emphasizing her rejection not only of Victorianism but of womanhood.

34. Osborn Collection, Box Number 47, Holograph sheet in paper folder in envelope labeled "Bits of The Moonlight."

35. Wright, *Joyce Cary*, p. 69.

36. Osborn Collection, Box Number 47, Holograph sheet in orange-covered, medium-sized notebook labeled "Moon."

37. Joyce Cary, *A Fearful Joy*, p. 5. Subsequent page references are to this Carfax edition.

38. Variations on this theme of the heiress or supposed heiress falling in love with a worthless man who marries her for her money can be found among Cary's unpublished manuscripts, including a radically different version of *Facts of Life*. In this version Clara Wendt, three times divorced, is "the rich girl who elopes with her father's chauffeur to learn the facts of life, and to get away from family prayers, Victorian morality . . . and ending up more or less on the streets." (Osborn Collection, Box Number 107, Typescript sheet in manuscript bundle labeled in Wright's hand, "From box labelled in Cary's hand 'Short Novel *Facts of Life*.' ") Other fragments of stories using this theme are "Juno" and "The Homely Nurse," but it is the first version of *Facts of Life* and the old beginning of *A Fearful Joy* which are most closely and directly related to the novel.

39. Osborn Collection, Box Number 107, Typescript sheets 1, 2, and 3 in manuscript bundle labeled in Professor Wright's hand, "From box labelled in Cary's hand 'Short Novel *Facts of Life*.' " Contains cancellations. Betty Wendt is the heiress of her father's business, and for this reason Toner proposes to her. The family opposes the marriage, knowing Toner's reputation, but Betty is in love with Toner and rebels against the family.

40. Osborn Collection, Box Number 110, Typescript sheet in paper folder labeled "Its a gift" in manuscript bundle labeled "It's a gift." However, the first sheet in the paper folder is labeled, "Old begining [sic] of Fearful Joy. The Ball." This manuscript was published posthumously as a short story in *Texas Quarterly*, IV (Summer 1961), 74–83. However, since the manuscript version continues beyond the ending of the published story, I refer to the original manuscript in the Osborn Collection.

41. Osborn Collection, Box Number 110, Typescript sheet.

42. Ibid.

43. Osborn Collection, Box Number 244, Typescript sheet numbered 6 in paper folder labeled "Unfinished Novels BBC script."

44. The published version of "The Ball" ends with Tabitha on the verge of eloping with Bonser.

45. An interesting variation on the use of the present tense is found in a note for a story entitled "Song of Lally": "The girl (told like Mr. J) who whirls through life, love, marriage, etc & means all the time to ask what is happening to me, but never has time &—she thinks she'll have time when children gone & husband dead. But she feels then utterly confused and despairing—her brain too musty & memories remorse crowd upon her—even religion has gone from her—the memories come between—and then suddenly a summons from one of the children, can she help . . . she goes at once & is glad to get to work again." (Osborn Collection, Holograph sheet in unlabeled, large-sized, black-covered looseleaf notebook.) There are elements in this plot outline which are suggestive of *A Fearful Joy*, and it is possible that Cary made use of it when he came to write the novel.

46. Osborn Collection, Box Number 51, Holograph note in medium-sized, yellow-covered writing pad.

47. Osborn Collection, Box Number 54, Holograph sheet in medium-sized, tan-covered notebook labeled "F. J."

48. Osborn Collection, Box Number 54, Holograph sheet in medium-sized, tan-covered notebook labeled "F. J."

49. Ibid.

50. Osborn Collection, Box Number 54, Holograph sheet headed "Theme" in medium-sized, tan-covered notebook labeled "F. J."

CHAPTER VII

1. Osborn Collection, Box Number 61, Holograph sheet attached to inside cover of large-sized notebook labeled "Prisoners of Grace. N. & T."

2. Cary, "The Way a Novel Gets Written," p. 89.

3. Burrows and Hamilton, "Joyce Cary," p. 65.

4. Cary, "The Way a Novel Gets Written," pp. 89, 91.

5. In the *Paris Review* interview Cary specifically warns the critic against interpreting his works allegorically. Burrows and Hamilton, "Joyce Cary," p. 65.

6. Osborn Collection, Box Number 61, Typescript sheet, all in capital letters, in large-sized notebook. In this same

note Cary insists that Chester Nimmo is not Lloyd George: "I dont like novels which pretend to give the history of real people. I'd rather read real history. *I wanted a nonconformist because* of importance in liberal democratic history. And a poor man make [sic] his way and the type is very common among left politicians." Many of the typescript notes for the second trilogy are in whole or in part capitalized. Since the purpose of the capitalization seems simply to be for easier reading than for emphasis, I have not indicated the capitalization in the text. Cary regularly used underlining for emphasis in all his notes.

7. Joyce Cary, *Prisoner of Grace*, p. 5. Subsequent page references are to this Carfax edition.

8. Osborn Collection, Box Number 61, Typescript and Holograph sheet headed "Back Notes. Jan. 1950" in large-sized notebook.

9. Osborn Collection, Box Number 242, Typescript sheet 5 of preface to German edition of *Not Honour More*.

10. The second trilogy Cary states "began in a dialogue between two women, written in a notebook, I rather think somewhere in a train" (Osborn Collection, Box Number 244, Typescript sheet 6, "Unfinished Novels"). Cary describes this dialogue in considerable detail:

> There were two women, one called Aunt X and the other niece Y. Niece Y has been proposed to by an ambitious, young man in the village. She has refused him, she takes the whole thing as a joke and tells the Aunt about it. But the Aunt says, "You are a very silly girl, that young man is going to have a future and you haven't got any future as you are. You think you are so pretty and clever but your looks aren't going to last and your cleverness is simply in amusing yourself and dodging responsibility. As you are going now you will make a complete waste of your own life, but that young man would make something of you and give you a real career. What's more, he is very fond of you and will never let you down if he can help it" [Osborn Collection, Box Number 244, Typescript sheets 6–7, "Unfinished Novels." Contains a cancellation.]

This immediately and directly gave Cary the basic situation for *Prisoner of Grace* and the second trilogy:

I said at once, "Here is a good situation for my political novel. The ambitious young man will be my politician, the clever girl shall tell the story. What's more, since she does not love him and is pushed into marriage by Aunt X, she will have on her hands a political job, in handling a husband so different from herself in ideas, in character, and in taste" [Osborn Collection, Box Number 244, Typescript sheet 7, "Unfinished Novels." Contains cancellations.]

Cary's imagination seized upon this bit of dialogue, and the note ceased to be an isolated anecdote in a notebook and became the *donnée* of *Prisoner of Grace*, just as an anecdote about a legal squabble over the possessions of a house became for Henry James the *donnée* for *The Spoils of Poynton*.

11. Osborn Collection, Box Number 59, Typescript sheet in bundle labeled "Prisoner of Grace bits and pieces cuts etc."

12. Osborn Collection, Box Number 59, Typescript sheet in paper folder labeled "P of G. March. 1950 N.V." Contains a cancellation.

13. Cary, *Prisoner of Grace*, pp. 20–21. Note that the idea of marrying Nimmo comes later.

14. Osborn Collection, Box Number 61, Typescript sheet in large-sized notebook.

15. Osborn Collection, Box Number 61, Holograph sheet attached to inside cover of large-sized notebook labeled "Prisoners of Grace. N. & T." Note that original title was "Prisoners of Grace."

16. Ibid., Typescript sheet.

17. Osborn Collection, Box Number 61, Typescript sheet in paper folder containing Holograph notes on the first trilogy for the Carfax edition prefaces.

18. Osborn Collection, Box Number 58, Typescript sheet headed "Tom Final Notes."

19. Osborn Collection, Box Number 58, Typescript sheet headed "Tom and Chester." Note that in relation to this Cary wrote: "His art at end not wrong in itself but in its meanness i.e. artist is responsible for a moral direction." (Osborn Collection, Box Number 61, Typescript sheet headed "Back Notes" in large-sized notebook labeled "Prisoners of Grace. N. & T.")

20. Osborn Collection, Box Number 61, Typescript sheet

in paper folder containing Holograph notes on first trilogy prefaces.

21. Joyce Cary, *Except the Lord*, p. 214. Subsequent page references are to this edition.

22. Osborn Collection, Box Number 68, Typescript sheet in large-sized maroon-covered looseleaf notebook labeled "Except the L. Not H. More." The "I" of the note is not necessarily Cary himself, for he often assumed the role of his characters in making notes on them.

23. Osborn Collection, Box Number 66, gray-covered, small-sized notebook, unlabeled.

24. Cary, *Except the Lord*, p. 87. The play is "true" only in the sense that it is based on an actual murder case, the Murder in the Red Barn which took place in 1828, but the real circumstances were quite different from those represented in the play (see *Except the Lord*, p. 91). Yet for Nimmo the play is "true" in the larger sense of art and politics.

25. The closest parallel to this is the addition of the final chapter to *The African Witch*, but Cary made that addition before the manuscript was sent to the publisher.

26. This letter is quoted with the kind permission of Mr. Roland Gant and of Michael Joseph, Ltd. The reference to Walter Allen is to Mr. Allen's reader's report to Michael Joseph in which he suggested that Cary make clear at the very beginning of *Except the Lord* its relationship to *Prisoner of Grace* since it is intended as the second novel of a trilogy. The letter was typed by Cary himself, and since Cary's typing was very poor, I have corrected obvious typographical errors in the text. The exact copy of the letter follows:

Oxford Sunday 2/53

Dear Lusty,

the form od the book is good and the proof are btter than usual but I am much dissatiesfied with my own work, especlly at the beginning, so I an doing a good deal of re-writng in the fisrst chpater. it will make *all the diff3rence* believe me to the book.

But I am taking the greatest trouble to avoid overrunning at scuch a place or too much cutting. If htere is too much or too l it tel material material anywhere , let the printer phone me at once and ill sttle the thing. It will be only the matter of a word ar two in any case to fill out a paragraph or sqaure off a chapter.

Ill send these first vital corrections at once as soon as thea are done so that difficulties can be snarled out.

Can you let me have another proof copy for the states - I a m making rather a mess of the one I have as ti saves time yo cut on thepage.

I earnestly assure you that this work on the first chapterw trsnsfrom s the book. Walter allen was obviously worried about em and I saw what he meant as ssoon as I saw the proof½

Yours ever,

(signed) Joyce Cary

27. Osborn Collection, Box Number 64, Typescript sheet numbered A 1. This passage is canceled out on the sheet and the following note appended: "this in the later chapter."

28. Osborn Collection, Box Number 65, Typescript sheet numbered 1 in paper folder labeled "XCT I T. S. March." Compare this with the published text: "Yesterday, an old man nearing my end, I stood by the grave of a noble woman, one of the three noblest I have ever known, my mother, my sister, my wife. If I draw back now the curtain from my family life, sacred to memory, I do so only to honour the dead, and in the conviction that my story throws light upon the crisis that so fearfully shakes our whole civilization" (*Except the Lord*, p. 5).

29. Page proof of *Except the Lord* at the Bodley, Cary A. 68 in the Bodleian hand list. The catalogue number is erroneously listed as A. 48 in Wright's *Hand List*.

30. Ibid.

31. Joyce Cary, *Not Honour More*, p. 1. Subsequent page references are to this edition.

32. Osborn Collection, Box Number 68, Typescript sheet dated July, 1953, and headed "Honour More" in large-sized, maroon-covered looseleaf notebook labeled "Except the L. Not H. More." Such precise dating of notes and manuscript

versions is, unfortunately, extremely rare in the manuscript collection.

33. Osborn Collection, Box Number 68, Typescript sheet dated September, 1952.

34. Wright, *Joyce Cary*, p. 149.

35. "A Lesser Cary," *Nation*, 181 (October 15, 1955), 328.

36. This theme, the relation of "truth" to "fact" as reported in the newspapers, is explored more fully and deeply in Cary's last novel, *The Captive and the Free*.

37. Osborn Collection, Box Number 67, Holograph note on outside cover of paper folder labeled "N. H. M. 8."

CHAPTER VIII

1. Joyce Cary, *The Captive and the Free*, p. 5. Subsequent page references are to this edition.

2. The following lines, found in the final manuscript version Joyce Cary made but canceled by Mrs. Davin in the penultimate typescript of the novel, continue where the published text leaves off:

> They had reached the office. Hooper, excited, full of triumph, turned to Joanna "You'll go on home, will you"
> She didn't answer.
> The photographer jumped out & Hooper followed. But as he closed the door, he felt a sudden resentment against this. . . ."

The manuscript breaks off at this point. Osborn Collection, Box Number 73, Holograph sheet in paper folder labeled "C & F January."

3. Osborn Collection, Box Number 74, Typescript sheet headed "*Captive and Free*" in large-sized, dark green folder labeled "C and F." Contains cancellations.

4. Cary, *Aissa Saved*, p. 8.

5. Cary, *First Trilogy*, p. xiv.

6. Ibid. Cary wrote this preface only a few weeks before his death.

7. The narrator of *The Captive and the Free* is simply identified as "we" in the published text, but in the manuscript

Cary further identified the narrator as one of Syson's parishioners. The last paragraph of the first chapter reads as follows in the manuscript: "This seemed to some of us in the parish a fearful injustice because there was something to be said for the poor devil. We think he had bad luck. We'll admit that he is, as the judge remarked, a hasty man. But he did not mean to cause trouble at Pant's Road, far from it, he was very anxious not to cause trouble." (Osborn Collection, Box Number 73, Typescript sheet 1 in paper folder labeled "C & F January.") Mrs. Davin wisely decided to eliminate this identification of narrator not only because it seems somewhat obtrusive at this point, but also because it tends to weaken the detachment and impersonality of the narrator by identifying him with Syson even though the narrator is actually quite neutral in the controversy.

8. Osborn Collection, Box Number 276, Typescript sheet 5 of article labeled in Edith Millen's hand "Article on Author's Religious history."

9. Osborn Collection, Box Number 276, Typescript sheet 6.

10. Osborn Collection, Box Number 276, Typescript sheet 11.

11. Cary, *The Captive and the Free*, p. 7. Ironically, when the story broke in the newspapers that Joyce Cary had muscular atrophy, incurable and fatal, he received letters from believers in faith-healing. The first letter is dated "27–8–56" and reads as follows:

Dear Mr. Cary,

I have read about you in today's Daily Express. As there is no cure in medical science for the disease which you believe is slowly destroying your body I would suggest that you should write to our friend Brother Mandus, 476 Lytham Road, Blackpool, Lancs, and ask him to call and see you as soon as possible. . . .

Brother Mandus is a consecrated channel for divine healing, and during the last few years he has healed people just as hopelessly ill as you seem to be: so there is a possibility that you, too, can be brought back to health and normality. I think you would be wise to contact him; and if you were not healed you would be no worse through his ministration, and almost certainly you would be blessed in some way.

Sincerely yours,

(signed)

(Osborn Collection, Box Number 75, Holograph letter in large beige folder labeled "C. and F. Final Notes.") The second letter is clipped together with the above letter and is dated "6th Sept '56":

Dear Mr. Cary,

I am so sorry to hear of your illness.

I have put your name on the distant healing list of the Glasgow Psychic Healing Centre of which I am a member and from which I myself have received great benefit. . . .

You believe in God and with God all things are possible. Miracles are brought about by the working of laws that we do not yet understand.

Sincerely yours,

(signed)

That he was writing a novel about faith-healing at this time is an irony that Joyce Cary, whose novels explore the irony of life, would fully understand.

12. Osborn Collection, Box Number 72, Typescript sheets 1 in paper folder labeled "C. and F. First version." In this version the faith-healer, who convinced Mrs. Croyd to bring her dying child to him, is named Parkin. Cary makes use of this incident in a much revised form near the end of the final version, the crucial scene involving Ada Rollwright whose death leads to Preedy's downfall.

13. Osborn Collection, Box Number 72, Typescript sheet in paper folder labeled "C and F (1955–6 early draught: variation of old beginning."

14. Osborn Collection, Box Number 72, Typescript sheets in unlabeled paper folder. Ann, by falling in love with Preedy, serves the function of Alice in the published version.

15. Osborn Collection, Box Number 75, Typescript sheets in large black looseleaf notebooks labeled "Case."

16. Osborn Collection, Box Number 75, Typescript sheet headed "C. and F." in unlabeled large green looseleaf notebook.

17. Osborn Collection, Box Number 74, Holograph sheet in large dark green folder labeled "C and F."

18. Osborn Collection, medium-sized notebook labeled "T. M. L. [i.e. *Teach Me to Live*]."

BIBLIOGRAPHY

MANUSCRIPTS

The James M. Osborn Collection of Joyce Cary Manuscripts, Bodleian Library, Oxford, England.

NOVELS

The Carfax edition of Joyce Cary's Novels (London, Michael Joseph), in order as mentioned in the notes.

Aissa Saved, 1952.	*A House of Children*, 1951.
An American Visitor, 1952.	*Herself Surprised*, 1951.
The African Witch, 1951.	*To Be a Pilgrim*, 1951.
Castle Corner, 1952.	*The Horse's Mouth*, 1951.
Mister Johnson, 1952.	*The Moonlight*, 1952.
Charley Is My Darling, 1951.	*A Fearful Joy*, 1952.

Prisoner of Grace, 1954.

The Horse's Mouth. Ed. Andrew Wright. London, George Rainbird in association with Michael Joseph, 1957.

First Trilogy. New York, Harper & Row, 1958.

Except the Lord. London, Michael Joseph, 1953.

Not Honour More. New York, Harper & Row, 1955.

The Captive and the Free. London, Michael Joseph, 1959.

SHORT FICTION

"Dinner at the Beeders'" (excerpt of *The Horse's Mouth*). *Harper's*, CXCIX (September 1949), 38–46.

"The Old Strife at Plant's" (a discarded chapter of *The Horse's Mouth*) *Harper's*, CCI (August 1950), 80–96; Oxford, privately printed with illustrations by the author, 1956.

"The Ball" (discarded beginning of *A Fearful Joy*) *Texas Quarterly*, IV (Summer 1961), 74–83.

ESSAYS

Art and Reality (the Clark Lectures 1956). New York, Harper, 1958.

"Important Authors of the Fall, Speaking for Themselves." *New York Herald-Tribune Book Review*, October 8, 1950, p. 10.

"An Interview with Joyce Cary, conducted by John Burrows and Alex Hamilton." *Paris Review*, VIII (Winter 1954–55), 63–78. Reprinted in *Writers at Work: The "Paris Review" Interviews*. Ed. Malcolm Cowley. New York, 1958.

"My First Novel." *Listener*, April 16, 1953, pp. 637, 638.

"A Novel Is a Novel Is a Novel." *New York Times Book Review*, April 30, 1950, pp. 1, 34.

"A Novelist and His Public." *Listener*, September 30, 1954, pp. 521, 522.

"The Novelist at Work: A Conversation Between Joyce Cary and Lord David Cecil." *Adam International Review*, XVIII, nos. 212–13 (November–December 1950), 15–25.

"On the Function of the Novelist." *New York Times Book Review*, October 30, 1949, pp. 1, 52.

"The Period Novel." *Spectator*, November 21, 1952, p. 684.

Power in Men. Ed. Hazard Adams. Seattle, University of Washington Press, 1963.

"The Way a Novel Gets Written." *Harper's*, CC (February 1950), 87–93.

SELECTED SECONDARY SOURCES

Adam International Review, XVIII, nos. 212–213 (November–December 1950).

Adams, Hazard. "Blake and Gulley Jimson: English Symbolists." *Critique*, III, i, 3–14.

―――. "Joyce Cary's Three Speakers." *Modern Fiction Studies*, V, 108–20.

Allen, Walter Ernest. *Joyce Cary*. (Bibliographical Series of Supplements to *British Book News*.) London, Longmans, Green, 1958.

Bettman, Elizabeth R. "Joyce Cary and the Problem of Political Morality." *Antioch Review*, XVII (1957), 266–72.

Bloom, Robert. *The Indeterminate World: A Study of the Novels of Joyce Cary.* Philadelphia, University of Pennsylvania Press, 1962.

Bowen, Elizabeth. "An Old Chap." *Tatler,* November 4, 1942, p. 152.

Collins, Harold R. "Joyce Cary's Troublesome Africans." *Antioch Review,* XIII (1953), 397–406.

Craig, David. "Idea and Imagination: A Study of Joyce Cary." *Fox.* (Published by Aberdeen University Classical, Literary and Philosophical Societies.) N.d. (ca. 1954), pp. 3–10.

Hardy, Barbara. "Form in Joyce Cary's Novels." *Essays in Criticism,* IV (1954), 180–90.

Hoffmann, Charles G. "Joyce Cary and the Comic Mask." *Western Humanities Review,* XIII (Spring 1959), 135–42.

————. "Joyce Cary: Art and Reality. The Interaction of Form and Narrator." *University of Kansas City Review,* XXVI (June 1960), 273–82.

————. "'The Captive and the Free': Joyce Cary's Unfinished Trilogy." *Texas Studies in Literature and Language,* V (Spring 1963), 17–24.

————. "Joyce Cary's African Novels: 'There's a War On.'" *South Atlantic Quarterly,* LXII (Spring 1963), 229–43.

————. "The Genesis and Development of Joyce Cary's First Trilogy." *PMLA,* LXXVIII (September 1963), 431–39.

————. "'They Want To Be Happy': Joyce Cary's Unfinished *Castle Corner* Series." *Modern Fiction Studies,* IX (Autumn 1963), 217–25.

Johnson, Pamela Hansford. "Three Novelists and the Drawing of Character: C. P. Snow, Joyce Cary and Ivy Compton-Burnett." *Essays and Studies by Members of the English Association,* N.S. III (1950), 89–91.

Karl, Frederick R. "Joyce Cary: The Moralist as Novelist." *Twentieth Century Literature,* V, 183–96.

Kerr, Elizabeth M. "Joyce Cary's Second Trilogy." *University of Toronto Quarterly,* XXIX, 310–25.

Kettle, Arnold. *An Introduction to the English Novel,* II. London, 1953, pp. 177–84.

Modern Fiction Studies, IX, no. 3 (Autumn 1963).

Prescott, Orville. "Two Modern Masters: Cozzens, Cary." *In My Opinion*. Indianapolis, Bobbs-Merrill, 1952, pp. 180–99.

Ryan, Marjorie. "An Interpretation of Joyce Cary's *The Horse's Mouth*." *Critique*, II, i, 29–38.

Van Horn, Ruth G. "Freedom and Imagination in the Novels of Joyce Cary." *Midwest Journal*, V (1952–53), 19–30.

West, Anthony. "Books: Footloose and Fancy-Free." *New Yorker*, XXXVI (April 30, 1960), 170–76.

Woodcock, George. "Citizens of Babel: A Study of Joyce Cary." *Queens Quarterly*, LXIII (1956), 236–46.

Wright, Andrew. *Joyce Cary: A Preface to His Novels*. London, Chatto & Windus, 1958.

INDEX

Adams, Hazard, x
African novels, 1–4, 8–43, 44, 45, 47, 52–53, 106
The African Witch, x, 3, 11, 17, 25–34, 35, 42, 44, 52, 158
Aissa Saved, 2, 3, 8–18, 22, 23, 25, 26, 31, 32, 33, 34, 38, 42, 44, 63, 158, 162
Aladé, 25, 26, 27, 28
Alexandria Quartet, 2, 5, 7
Allen, Walter, x, 144, 192–93n
An American Visitor, 3, 17, 18–25, 33, 34, 38, 42, 44, 45, 52
Appearance and reality, 48–49, 130, 150, 151, 152–55, 163, 165–66, 169
Arabella, 53, 177–80n
Art and freedom, 58–59, 60, 75, 86–89, 92, 94, 96, 137, 158, 159
Art and Reality, 55, 68
Art and religion, 5, 75–76, 92, 131, 159, 160–61
Art and society, 67, 69, 76, 86–87, 88–89, 90, 94, 137–38
Artist as God, 76, 93–95, 96, 138, 185n
Autobiographical novel, 55–57, 60, 140

"The Ball," 118–21
Balzac, Honoré de, 2, 3
Bennett, Arnold, 4
Blake, William, 1, 75, 86, 87, 89, 90–93, 94–95, 97, 160
Bloom, Robert, x, 24–25
Bodleian Library, ix, x, 2
Bow Down to Heaven, 99

The Captive and the Free (incomplete and unpublished trilogy), 5, 6, 99–107

The Captive and the Free (posthumous novel), 6, 137, 157–69
Cary, Arthur Pitt (Cary's father), 49
Cary manuscripts. *See* Osborn Collection
Castle Corner, 3, 18, 34, 44–53, 54–57, 106–07, 124, 128
Castle Corner series, 1, 2, 3, 4, 45–53, 54–55, 105–06, 148
Cecil, Lord David, 157, 159–61
Central observer, 121, 134, 165, 166
Chance, 5
Change: as the condition of freedom, 1, 2, 48, 78–80, 89–90, 125–26
Charley Is My Darling, 53, 54–66, 137
Clayhanger, 4
Clea, 7
Cock Jarvis, 51–52, 55
"Comedy of Freedom" (abandoned title for general preface to Carfax edition), 1
Comedy of freedom, 1, 37–38, 169
Conflict of artist and society. *See* Art and society
Conrad, Joseph, 5, 12, 23, 24, 44, 68, 134

Daventry, 172–73n
Detached author, 15, 24–25, 28, 159, 162
Davin, Winifred (Mrs.), ix, x, 147, 157, 164, 194n, 195n
Durrell, Lawrence, 2, 5, 6, 7

Easy Money, 6, 99, 100–01, 104
Except the Lord, xi, 5, 128, 130–31, 132, 139–47, 149, 151, 156

Facts of Life, 118–21, 188n
Faith: crisis of; renewal. *See* conversion and salvation under Themes
Family chronicle, 2, 3, 4, 45, 50, 105, 128, 148
A Fearful Joy, 35, 99, 104, 105, 106, 107, 118–26, 128, 148–49
Finnegan's Wake, 68
Form. *See* Narrator
Forster, E. M., 27, 28–29, 81, 83
Forsyte Saga, 2, 4
Fall into freedom, 73–74, 92–93, 95–96
Freedom
  and the creative imagination, 38, 54, 58–59, 71, 86–89, 91, 92, 94–95, 135, 137–38, 158, 169
  for evil and good, 1, 48, 86, 138, 154, 161
  limited by responsibility, 1, 32, 49, 80, 81, 106, 109, 132, 138–39, 158, 163, 167

Galsworthy, John, 2, 4
Grace and forgiveness, 49, 67, 71, 74, 77, 94, 96–97, 130, 136, 137, 141, 148, 149, 150, 151, 155, 156, 163
Green Jerusalem, 3, 46, 51, 52, 176–77n

Hardy, Barbara, x, 6
Hardy, Thomas, 12
Herself Surprised, 4, 5, 7, 66, 67, 68, 70–77, 80, 85, 93, 104–05, 127, 137, 139, 152, 163
Honor, concept of, 132, 136, 142, 149–50, 151, 152, 154, 155
A House of Children, 53, 54–66
Howard's End, 81, 83

Huxley, Aldous, 14, 24, 28
The Horse's Mouth, 5, 7, 66, 67, 68, 69, 71, 72, 74, 77, 79, 85–98, 132, 134, 137, 150, 152, 158, 159, 163

Idealism, 20–23, 24, 30, 33, 38, 144
Impressionism, 87
"Indeterminateness," x, 24–25, 173n
Injustice: as the condition of freedom, 87–88, 97, 105–06, 109, 116, 147, 154, 161–62, 163, 169

James, Henry, 12–13, 68
Jimson trilogy, x, 4–5, 6–7, 66, 67–98, 132, 134, 137–38, 150, 158
Joyce, James, 35, 68, 91

Keats, John, 25
Kreutzer Sonata, 107–09, 117

La Comèdie Humaine (Honoré de Balzac), 2, 3
Lawrence, D. H., 91, 111
Lord Jim, 23, 134

Mansfield, Katherine, 64–65
Marta, 53, 178–80n
"The Mental Traveller," 91
"Milton," 90
Mister Johnson, 17–18, 34–43, 44, 52–54, 58, 66, 124, 137
Mister Tottenham, Victim of Love, 180–81n
The Moonlight, x, 83, 99, 104, 105, 106, 107–18, 124, 125
Mrs. Dalloway, 35
The Music of Time, 2
Multiple novel form, 1–4, 6, 47, 53
Multiple view of reality, x, 2, 4–5, 7, 14, 25, 98, 128, 133, 134
"My First Ball," 64–65

Narrator
  first person, 4, 5, 53, 55–57,
    60–64, 66, 67–68, 88, 97–98,
    99, 101, 129–30, 131–32, 133–
    35, 152
  impersonal, detached, 4, 18,
    20, 23–24, 25, 28, 34, 36, 101,
    134, 165
  interaction with form, 4, 134,
    150–52
  multiple, 4–5, 7, 68
  single, 2, 7, 68
  third person, 4–5, 6, 19, 28, 34,
    55, 57, 99, 101, 159, 164
Negative capability, 25, 28, 67
Nimmo trilogy, 5, 6, 45, 100–03,
  104, 105, 127–56, 158, 159, 163
Novel of ideas, 25
Not Honour More, 5, 6, 45, 103,
  104, 128, 131, 132, 141, 144,
  148–56, 163, 165, 166

Organic method, 8–9
Orpheus-Eurydice myth, 96–97
Osborn, James M., Collection,
  ix–xi, 2, 3, 4, 5, 46, 51, 99, 149,
  157
Over the Top, 3, 46, 47–49, 51,
  52, 176–77n

Partial view of reality, 6, 14, 55,
  71–72, 132, 150, 152–53, 165
Passage to India, 27, 28, 29
Past tense (use), 35, 61, 107
Point Counter Point, 14
Point of view, 2, 4–5, 6, 14, 18,
  53, 57, 60, 66, 67, 68, 97, 101,
  117, 131, 134–35, 139, 151, 164,
  165, 166
Politics and religion, 11–12, 13,
  19, 68, 69, 128, 131, 136, 142–43
*Portrait of the Artist as a
  Young Man*, 35, 91
Post-Impressionism, 87
Powell, Anthony, 2, 7

Present tense (use), 17, 34–38,
  53, 54, 107, 121–22, 125, 148–49
Prisoner of Grace, 6, 100–02,
  104–05, 127, 128, 129, 130, 131,
  132, 133–39, 141, 142, 143, 145,
  148, 151, 152, 156, 163
Proust, Marcel, 7, 61

Racial prejudice, 20–21, 26–29,
  33–34, 40
The Rainbow, 111
Religious views (Cary), 159–61
Rougon-Macquart, 2
Ruskin, John, 87

Schorer, Mark, 34–35, 171n
Science and religion, 13–14, 15
Snow, C. P., 2, 7
"Song of Lally," 189n
Sons and Lovers, 91, 111
Strangers and Brothers, 2
Stream of consciousness tech-
  nique, 35, 86
Structure, 2, 3, 4, 50, 69, 74, 83,
  85, 89, 98, 117, 140, 147, 150,
  152–55
Symbols
  Castle Corner, 3, 46–47, 50, 55
  cave, 96
  clothes, 26, 29–31, 37
  "The Creation," 89, 95–97
  "The Fall," 89, 90–93
  fish, 95–96
  moonlight, 109, 112–16, 118
  "The Raising of Lazarus,"
    89, 93–95
  roads and road building, 16–
    17, 38–40
  she-whale, 95–96
  Tolbrook Farm, 47, 79, 81–85

"Theirs is the Kingdom" (rejected title for *Aissa Saved*),
  14
Themes
  the captive and the free, 105–
    06, 107, 157–69

Themes (*Continued*)

   change, 1, 3, 23–24, 44–45, 46–47, 48, 50, 65, 67, 70, 71, 72, 78–80, 81, 82–85, 105–06, 107, 111, 116–17, 118, 121–24, 125–26, 128, 136–37, 138, 168

   the child is a born creator, 54–66

   conversion and salvation of a lost soul, 10–11, 81, 82, 95, 96, 125, 130–31, 140–42, 143–44, 147, 149, 159, 161, 162–64, 167–68, 169

   creative renewal, 96, 97, 115, 118, 122–23, 125–26, 147

   freedom as perpetual creation, 1, 3, 70, 85, 86–88, 89–90, 92, 95, 96, 97, 123, 159

   love and sacrifice, 10–11, 14–15, 22–23, 33, 42, 109–12, 117–18, 155

   love as a fearful joy, 99, 107–26

   politics as the art of human relations, 127–56

   war between incompatible ideals, 2–3, 10, 14, 15–18, 19, 22–25, 28, 34, 42–45, 46–47, 50, 51, 55, 106, 124, 155, 159–60, 162

Three "voices," x, 4, 5, 67

To the Lighthouse, 83, 150

To Be a Pilgrim, x, 4, 5, 7, 47, 51, 67, 68, 69, 71, 72, 74, 77–85, 93, 128, 131, 135, 140, 142, 152, 159

Tolstoy, Leo, 107–08, 110, 111, 117

Trilogy form, 2, 4–6, 18, 47, 60, 66, 67–70, 77, 97–98, 99–100, 107, 127–28, 131–32, 133, 134, 150

Triptych, 4, 5, 7, 68–70, 77, 127–28, 150

"The Way a Novel Gets Written," 128

West, Anthony, 57–58

Woolf, Virginia, 35, 83, 150

Wright, Andrew, x, 19, 46, 116, 150–51

Zola, Emile, 2